BUILDING OO GAUGE
Wagons and Vans
FOR MODEL RAILWAYS

BUILDING OO GAUGE
Wagons and Vans
FOR MODEL RAILWAYS

DAVID TISDALE

THE CROWOOD PRESS

First published in 2015 by
The Crowood Press Ltd
Ramsbury, Marlborough
Wiltshire SN8 2HR

www.crowood.com

British Library Cataloguing-in-Publication Data
A catalogue record for this book is available from the British Library.

ISBN 978 1 84797 983 4

Disclaimer
The author and the publisher do not accept any responsibility in any manner whatsoever for any error or omission, or any loss, damage, injury, adverse outcome, or liability of any kind incurred as a result of the use of any of the information contained in this book, or reliance upon it. If in doubt about any aspect of railway modelling readers are advised to seek professional advice.

Typeset by Servis Filmsetting Ltd, Stockport, Cheshire
Printed and bound in Malaysia by Times Offset (M) Sdn Bhd

CONTENTS

DEDICATION

I would like to dedicate this book to my family for tolerating my model railway stuff all over the house and especially to my understanding and loving wife Tracey – thank you for the support and encouragement during the preparation of this book.

PREFACE

The idea for writing this book came to me whilst writing short magazine articles about the construction of a number of pieces of rolling stock. It seemed to me that there was not a simple, single source text on the subject that a newcomer to the hobby, or someone wanting to think beyond just ready-to-run and kit building, could turn to for ideas and guidance. An opportunity presented itself when by accident I came across a note in one of the popular monthly railway magazines to contact The Crowood Press if you had an idea for a book on model railways. A preliminary exchange of letters and emails ensued, followed by the submission of a book proposal, which was accepted and this book is the end result. I hope the book lives up to my original concept idea.

ACKNOWLEDGEMENTS

I would like to convey my thanks to my fellow railway modellers at the Jersey Model Railway Club for their support, advice and encouragement over the past few years that I have been a member.

As a railway modeller, a builder of kits and a scratch builder, I would like to give a special mention to the numerous dedicated and enthusiastic suppliers of kits and components on whom I and many others rely for supplies to feed our hobby. Without these people the railway modelling hobby would be a poorer place, so thank you for your industry and long may it continue.

CHAPTER ONE

WHY BUILD YOUR OWN ROLLING STOCK?

READY-TO-RUN OR BUILD-YOUR-OWN?

Given the quality of OO gauge ready-to-run (RTR) models available today from the likes of Bachmann, Dapol, Heljan and Hornby, where the level of fine detail is excellent, you might well ask why build your own rolling stock? You might also question as to whether you can achieve the same level of detail, running quality and overall finish to the model as can be achieved by the commercial manufacturers.

The answers depend on the level of skill and patience applied to the process. For me, the development of skills with practice gives me a great sense of satisfaction, when I have created something myself, rather than buying it from the shop, lifting it out of the box and playing with it. It is a sense of achievement to create something and, in my case, I enjoy striving to produce as high a quality model as my limited skills afford.

I have been asked a number of times over the years as to why I should want to build my own rolling stock when, especially in the last five to ten years, the quality of the RTR models on the market is very good. The answer is, I think, that it is the desire to create some examples of rolling stock that are not readily available as RTR models and the desire to have something just that little bit different or unique running on my layout.

TRAIN SET TO MODEL RAILWAY

Many of us, I am sure, will have been initiated to the hobby by the childhood train set as a Christmas or birthday present set on a flat board, with a loco and a couple of carriages and wagons trundling around in a circle. If you were very lucky and had the space, you may have had the opportunity to construct a more extensive train set in a spare room or loft. Over time this develops with the addition of more track, sidings, maybe some buildings and the start of scenery, and very soon the train set starts to become a more serious model, which could be termed a model railway layout rather than a train set. Maybe as one develops from a train set, the application of additional details – loads for wagons, weathering, etc. – to RTR items is the first step down the road to building your own rolling stock.

The first step commonly taken after the train set stage is to look to build a layout that is a little more realistic, or representative, of your chosen railway company, geographical area of country, or specific operation or activity served by a railway. It is at this stage that it usually becomes apparent that the rolling stock produced by the RTR manufacturers might not meet your requirements.

The RTR range of models may not have all the necessary examples of rolling stock that would be relevant to the period being modelled, the area that you are trying to create or a specific industrial use, and thus kit building becomes the favoured option. In fact thinking about it, the next logical extension of the development of your model railway after creating the scenery, permanent way and buildings or structures, is to put your own interpretation and skill in to the rolling stock to run on the layout.

The model railway press regularly includes articles about building kits, converting ready-to-run models and scratch building rolling stock, and these can be a source of inspiration and guidance for those considering undertaking any of these projects.

BUILDING YOUR OWN ROLLING STOCK

In the following chapters I will consider the options available for building your own rolling stock, in the case of this book in terms of OO gauge, although the ideas and techniques discussed in this book can easily be applied to any scale/gauge combination. I have myself applied this to N gauge, OO9 and O-16.5 scale modelling, having built kits and scratch built rolling stock in all three of these scale/gauge combinations, using skills that I have learnt from my OO gauge modelling.

Before diving into the construction of kits, I will look at the selection of material types and some basic tool requirements in Chapter 2, and will provide some guidance as to what different material types can be used for different modelling tasks and what tools you should consider purchasing before embarking on creating your own rolling stock. Once you have assembled a basic toolkit and a supply of materials, component parts and kits, it is then time to begin.

KIT BUILDING

In Chapter 3, I will show, using worked examples, how you can move from building simple kits to more complicated kits in a variety of material types, including plastic, white metal and brass, similar to the range of kits shown in Figs 1 and 2. Kit building may not be everyone's cup of tea, but if you have the basic skills from putting together a model plane or tank kit, such as those produced by Airfix, then this need not be seen as a huge step up in ability.

Kit building provides the opportunity to develop and hone your modelling skills using commercially produced kits, typically in plastic (see Fig. 3) or metal (for example, white metal or brass) to develop your rolling stock inventory, as shown in the examples in Figs 4 and 5. Other examples of materials less commonly used for kits, including wood and resin, are discussed in more detail in Chapter 2.

Over time and with experience it will become apparent that even kit building has its limitations. This will be even more apparent if your chosen prototype era, locality, line-side industrial use or railway company is not one of the more widely known or

Fig. I Some examples of plastic wagon and van kits available for the modeller as currently produced kits or available second-hand.

Fig. 2   Examples of etched brass kits currently available for the modeller to build, or use as replacement parts to plastic kits.

Fig. 3   A typical example of an extruded plastic wagon kit, in this case requiring the modeller to provide paint, decals and wheels to complete.

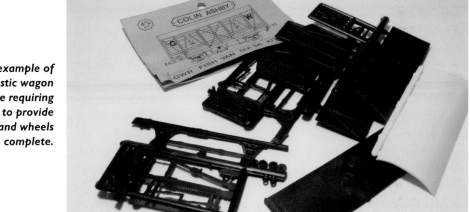

Fig. 4   An example of relatively simple white metal open wagon kit, with etched brass fine detail components and plasticard sections for the floor.

Fig. 5   Etched brass wagon kits available from manufacturers such as Falcon Brassworks, are typically provided with white metal components and for the modeller to provide wheels.

supported examples in terms of trade suppliers of kits and components.

KIT DETAILING AND CONVERSION

The next logical step after kit building is to detail and convert (often referred to as kit bashing) existing kits and then to consider the ultimate in rolling stock construction: scratch building. So what is kit conversion and scratch building? Well kit conversion, I would define, although I am sure not all would agree, is where you take an available model kit similar to

the prototype you are looking to create and then modify it significantly to produce a model of the exact prototype you wish to create.

This is different from detailing a kit where you are sticking with the original prototype on which the kit is based and maybe adding additional details that the kit does not include; for example, fitting the correct pattern of wagon buffers (a common problem in some commercially produced kits) or adding wagon loads and tarpaulins.

Fig. 6   Adding detail to a plastic van kit, including the underframe and brake gear as shown here, greatly enhances the basic kit.

Fig. 7   Using a variety of materials, including brass sheet, plasticard and wire, it is possible to scratch build a reasonable representation of a bogie goods van.

In Chapter 4, I will look at detailing kits, working through an example of what can be achieved with detailing a van kit (see Fig. 6) and I will provide hints and tips as to what may or may not be possible. I will also look at the creation of different types of loads for open wagons and how these can be covered and secured.

In Chapter 5, I will discuss the options available for the conversion of kits, as well as the possibilities for converting RTR models, using some worked examples of conversions that I have carried out, to provide a guide to the possible methods and techniques that can be employed.

SCRATCH BUILDING

Scratch building is another area where there is likely to be some dispute over the definition, so to avoid controversy and protracted debate, I will provide my own definition here as the basis on which this book has been put together and leave it to the reader to decide whether this sits comfortably with them or not. To my mind scratch building is the creation of a model of a prototype from scratch using the 'raw' materials (see Chapter 2) with or without the use of small component parts; for example, the use of etched brass wagon strapping or 'W' irons.

In Chapters 6 and 7, I will look at what can be achieved by scratch building rolling stock and will show that this need not necessarily be the preserve of the highly skilled or professional modeller. I will discuss in Chapter 6 the use of materials and techniques that can be used for scratch building; whilst in Chapter 7, I will provide a number of worked examples of scratch building to demonstrate what can be achieved with the application of research, patience and modelling skills. One of the examples I have described is the scratch building of a bogie goods van using plasticard and brass, which shows what can be achieved in these materials.

To aid the scratch builder, there is a plethora of suppliers around today that can provide all sorts of small component parts that will save the scratch builder from having to fabricate every tiny piece of detail for a particular prototype subject being modelled. Having said that, I see no problem, if you feel you have the time, desire, skill level and tools to do the job, with fabricating all these components yourself.

Now having set the scene, it is time to get on with the modelling and I hope that the hints, tips and worked examples presented in this book provide a useful reference for you to develop your modelling skills and will inspire you to have a go.

CHAPTER TWO

KITS, MATERIALS AND TOOLS

INTRODUCTION

Before we delve into the detail of kit building and scratch building rolling stock, I will provide a quick review and summary of the types of kits, materials and tools that are available today for the railway modeller to use. This subject has been covered many times before by others, so I plan to provide a brief summary and comments based on my own experience that will be of use to others starting out in this area.

I have found that the quality of kits and components can be extremely variable, and this is not always related to the cost of the items purchased. The production of kits and components for the railway modeller is an area of significant business, covering all the more common and less common railway companies, and through the pre-grouping, grouping, nationalization and privatization periods of British railway heritage.

I have not prepared an exhaustive list of suppliers of kits and components, as that would take a book

in its own right; suffice to say that there are many suppliers producing all manner of products to assist the modeller looking to build kits, modify RTR and kit built rolling stock or even scratch building. I have included a short list of the suppliers that I have used in my work in Appendix II, but I must emphasize that I have no connection to any of the suppliers listed, other than as a satisfied customer.

The best advice that I could provide to a beginner starting out would be to carry out some research on your prototype period, company and/or region, and then search the modelling press and internet, and visit railway exhibitions where traders are present, to see what is on offer, decide on what you need and, most importantly, what you can afford.

You might also wish to consider what you can fabricate from raw materials or adapt from spare parts from other kits. This depends on the level of accuracy of fine detail that you wish to achieve, but it is perfectly possible to create many components yourself using basic tools. There is no right or wrong answer, it is what you feel comfortable with

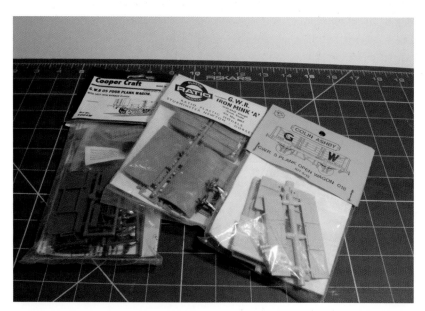

Fig. 8 For the beginner wanting to build wagon and van kits, a simple plastic kit, such as one from the selection shown, is a good place to start.

Fig. 9 Tackling a more complicated plastic kit, such as one of those shown here, provides more of a challenge to the budding rolling stock modeller.

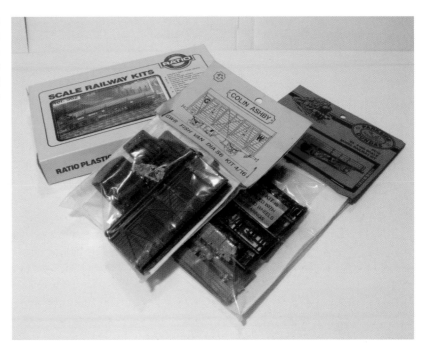

and what you have time to achieve (remember life is short!). Set out to achieve a realistic impression at moderate cost rather than set standards so high that you might be unable to attain them first time out. You can improve your skill levels and raise your standard with experience.

As a modeller you need to build up your skill levels and confidence, starting with more straightforward or simpler kits (see Fig. 8), then move to more complicated kits (see Fig. 9) as you develop your skills and confidence in your ability. It is important to remember when building a kit that you can always add more detail at a later date, if and when your skills or requirements for accuracy of finer detail have increased; you could see this as a future upgrade, a bit like the software and hardware for a home PC.

KITS AND MATERIALS

Beginning with kit types, the following provides a summary guide to the most common types of kits available, together with some comments based on my experiences of working with the material types employed.

PLASTIC

This medium is by far the most common material type used for model kit production at the present time. Typically this is extruded plastic derived using moulds to produce a range of parts and components to construct with liquid polystyrene cement. Plastic is a more forgiving material type to use than some materials, especially for the beginner, as it is relatively simple to correct mistakes or to fabricate a replacement part should anything untoward happen during the construction process.

These types of kits can be produced relatively cheaply, as compared to an etched brass kit, and consequently the price of these types of kits is less. The level of detail on early plastic kits was limited, but the more recent kits available from the likes of Parkside Dundas and Cambrian Models, to name but two suppliers, are significantly improved on earlier examples (see Fig. 11). The level of fine detail on many of the plastic kits available today is excellent and I find plastic kits are easy to work with and, having built many plastic model tanks, boats and aircraft kits as a child, it is the material I am most comfortable using and this is probably my favourite material type for building.

Fig. 10 Examples of basic plastic wagon and van kits such as these provide a useful source of kits for the modeller to develop model building skills.

Fig. 11 The kits shown here are examples of more complicated plastic kits available to the model rolling stock builder and require more advanced model building skills.

Fig. 12 Pre-printed wagon kits, such as the Ratio van kit, allow the modeller to provide examples of private owner rolling stock for their layout that may not be available RTR.

Fig. 13   The Slater's Plastikard range of pre-coloured open wagons, such as this coal wagon kit, is unfortunately only available second-hand at the time of writing.

An advantage of using plastic is that this can be produced in a variety of pre-coloured parts to help with the construction sequence or to represent colour schemes of the prototypes being modelled. One example of this type of flexibility is the older kits produced by Ratio, which unfortunately are no longer available new but it is possible to pick them up second-hand, to represent specific company brands, such as the Harvey's Bristol Cream wagon (see Fig. 12); a 10-ton van produced in company colours and pre-printed sides with the company branding.

Slater's OO gauge wagons, now produced under the Cooper Craft banner, also adopted a similar approach to the production of private owner wagons with pre-coloured body and printed sides for the company being represented (see Fig. 13). These wagon kits are relatively easy to make and with pre-coloured and printed sides mean that the keen modeller can have a train of private owner wagons built and running on the layout in a relatively short period of time, without worrying about identifying and applying the somewhat complicated liveries and branding used by some private organizations.

On the negative side, the one big disadvantage of using plastic is that the kits tend to be extremely light and, for good track adhesion and running, ballast will have to be added to all the models. To address the lightweight nature of plastic kits, some kit manufactures provide ballast weights with the kits, but some

do not. I have always added ballast, whether provided or not, using a combination of steel weights, white metal and even nails as ballast in wagons.

In vans or covered wagons this is easy to hide within the body. In open wagons this can be a little trickier, but some ballast can be hidden under the floor and some disguised and added in the form of wagon loads – you just have to use your imagination.

Many of the older plastic kits were also produced with plastic wheels; for example, the early Keyser plastic kits and early Cooper Craft kits. The use of plastic wheels only exacerbated the poor running problems of a lightweight body. The Keyser kits are no longer in production and the Cooper Craft kits have been upgraded and are now sold with metal wheel sets running in brass bearings. I have always fitted metal wheel sets to my kit-built wagons, typically using Keen Maygib, Romford or Alan Gibson fine-scale wheel sets running in brass bearings. It is relatively simple to adapt your wagon kit to take metal wheel sets; this will be discussed further in Chapters 3 and 4.

The cost of plastic kits, starting at around £7 for the more basic, simple wagon kit, is the ideal starting point for the beginner. My advice would be to consider plastic kits as a place to cut your teeth at kit building. Start with a simple four-wheel open wagon or box van; for example, the kits produced by Cooper Craft for Great Western rolling stock.

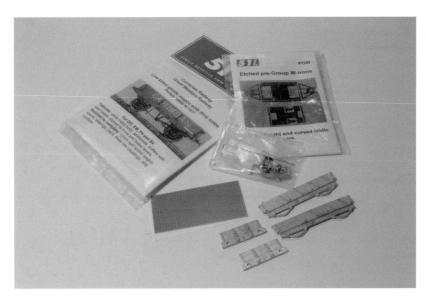

Fig. 14 *A simple white metal kit of a Cambrian Railway's slate wagon produced by 51L, is a good example of the type of kit available in this medium.*

These kits comprise only a few main components; a selection of detailed pieces and the new versions of the kits include a set of metal wheels and brass bearings to provide good running. Once you have mastered this type of kit, then graduate to the more complicated plastic kits and then the metal kits; this is discussed further in Chapter 3.

WHITE METAL

The use of white metal for producing kits was once more common, but has been replaced to a large degree by the developments in the production of extruded plastic kits. That is not to say that all white metal kit production has stopped – far from it. White metal kits are still available from some suppliers, such as ABS, 51L and David Green, particularly for the more obscure prototype wagons or, less commonly, modelled railway companies.

However, there is one area where white metal is still in common use: that is for the production of wagon components, as shown in Fig. 15. These types of components are used by the modeller looking to modify a kit to a different prototype, or the modeller considering scratch building. Suppliers, such as ABS, Mainly Trains, 51L and others, produce a wide range of parts to assist the railway modeller in this regard.

The level of detail available with both white metal kits and components can be variable and is governed by the quality of the mould used for the cast production. In my experience, some of the casting is excellent and is ready to use straight from the box or packet, whilst some requires a fair degree of fettling to remove flash and casting lines.

It is important to remember that white metal is a soft metal alloy and thus it is prone to easy damage or deformation from bending and even breakage if not handled carefully. It can be soldered using a low melt solder, but unless you are confident in your ability and competent at soldering, you do run the risk of your component or kit turning into a deformed molten lump, only good enough to use as ballast for your next plastic wagon kit! I tend to use an impact adhesive, such as UHU, or a cyanoacrylate adhesive (super glue) to bond white metal parts and kits, as I do not consider my soldering abilities are up to the mark for construction of these types of kits.

On the basis of my experience, the use of a liquid cyanoacrylate (super glue) type adhesive works extremely well with white metal, especially if you apply a small spot on the contact surfaces first, press together and then, once this sets, use a fine wire (such as a straightened paperclip) to apply more adhesive liquid to the join and allow capillary action to draw the liquid into the joint. Once left to harden off, I have found this approach provides a very strong joint.

Fig. 15 Detailing wagon and van kits can be achieved simply using white metal components, such as the selection of components available from ABS Models.

The main advantage of using white metal as the principal material for a wagon kit is that the wagons produced are much heavier and are unlikely to require additional ballast (as noted previously for plastic kits). This weight advantage, combined with the use of metal wheel sets, leads to good track adhesion and better running qualities for the rolling stock.

The key point to be aware of that I have found with the construction of white metal kits is that the construction process needs to be carried out carefully and progress checked regularly to ensure that the body is square and level. This applies to all types of kits, but more so with white metal, as the material is less flexible or readily adjusted once the joint has been fixed, without the risk that the parts might deform or break.

BRASS

The production of brass kits using etching techniques has been around for many years. For many people, the level of fine detail achievable, combined with the weight advantage over plastic kits, makes the brass kit the pinnacle of model building. The level of detail and degree of accuracy attainable from etched brass kit construction is excellent, although this all comes at a modest cost premium. Brass kits tend to be much more expensive than the equivalent

plastic kits and for someone starting out kit building, there is often the fear of spending a considerable sum of money on a kit and then ruining it by making a mistake that cannot be undone.

The skill level required for brass kit construction is higher and the kits tend to be more complicated than plastic or white metal kits. Having said all of this though, the modeller should not be put off from using brass kits. From my experience, it is better to start with the plastic and white metal kits and build up your modelling skills and understanding of how rolling stock kits are put together, before moving on to the brass kits.

Some suppliers produce part-brass components to modify existing plastic kits, whilst others produce brass body kits to fit on plastic underframes, such as the Shire Scenes range of etched brass bodies for wagons and four-wheel coaches designed to fit on to modified Ratio plastic coach chassis (*see* Fig. 17). These part-brass kits are probably a good place to start to get the feel of how to work with brass before moving on to the more complicated full-brass kits.

With brass kits it is essential to read through the instructions fully before commencing any construction and it is also advisable to carry out dry runs of key elements of the assembly process before fixing. This will be discussed in more detail later. Brass kits

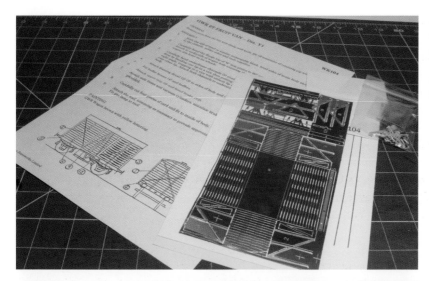

Fig. 16 An example of the type of etched brass kit available is the Great Western Railway fruit van kit produced by Falcon Brassworks.

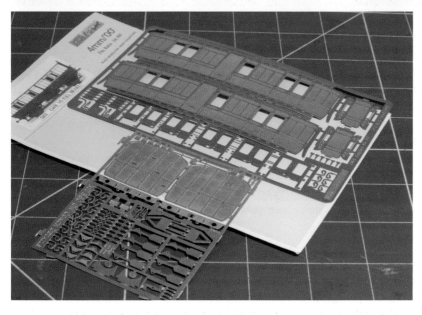

Fig. 17 A number of conversions for the Ratio plastic four-wheel coach kit can be achieved utilizing the Shire Scenes range of etched brass body kits.

can be fixed together by soldering or by the use of an adhesive, such as cyanoacrylate, depending on personal preference. Once constructed, brass kits provide strong models with a sufficient degree of weight that ensures excellent running qualities, especially when combined with good quality metal wheel sets.

RESIN

The use of resin for rolling stock construction provides an alternative to the use of plastic or metal.

Typically these types of kits are produced as a single cast of the body with a small number of parts for the underframe. Alternatively, resin kits are produced as a one-piece body casting designed to fit on a plastic underframe provided separately, or for the modeller to provide from a source of preference.

Resin is a light material and unless weights are cast into the body during the casting process, then the modeller needs to add ballast. Resin is popular amongst modellers who want to produce their own limited runs of a particular prototype. The level of detail achievable in resin kits can be the same as, if not better than, that achievable with extruded plastic kits. The quality of the casting, as with white metal, is governed by the quality of the mould.

Whilst I have not yet used resin kits for OO gauge wagons and vans, I have used resin kits for the construction of a fleet of London Underground tube and surface rolling stock for a friend and fellow modeller constructing a model of Gant's Hill Station. I have also used resin kits for the construction of O-16.5 rolling stock, running on OO gauge plastic underframe kits, for one of my own layouts at home.

WOOD

The use of wood as a base material type for constructing rolling stock is not common today in terms of commercially produced kits. Historically, wooden kits were produced by suppliers such as Ratio for wagons and carriages, but these have been superseded by the use of plastic. Although I have not constructed a rolling stock kit from wood, I have used wood as a material for the construction of parts of wagons, wagon loads, buildings and other scenic items for the model railway, including a scratch built Clyde Puffer to 4mm scale to sit in the harbour on the layout of a friend.

MATERIALS FOR SCRATCH BUILDING

There are no hard and fast rules about the choice of material for the project that you wish to undertake and in my opinion you should not rule anything in, or out, at the beginning until you have decided what your subject matter is going to be. It may, for example, be necessary to consider the use of a number of different material types in the same project to achieve the look and feel of the prototype that you intend from the model. I have used wood, plastic, metal and card for the projects that I have undertaken and each has its own advantages and disadvantages, a summary of which has been produced in the table Pros and Cons of Material Types.

For the construction of wagons and vans I have tended to use a mix of plasticard and brass sheet for the main body sections, whereas I have used plastic, brass and white metal to form the finer detailed components. Plasticard is readily workable to form the shape of the wagons, particularly the wagon and van ends, and this material can be sanded and carved as required. The brass sheets provide strength combined with a relatively thin profile and this has proved to be particularly useful for the formation of van roofs; for example, the roof of the GWR Mink F van described in more detail in Chapter 7.

MODELLERS' TOOLS FOR KIT BUILDING

Having looked at the range of material types available for kit building and scratch building, it is perhaps worth making some comment on the types of tools that would be beneficial for the modeller to have to hand before starting to construct your own rolling stock. To some degree the types of tools required vary for material types, but many are common to all material types, therefore I have approached this on the basis that the modeller requires tools to build kits.

BASIC TOOLS

For the modeller considering the construction of plastic or resin kits, the following basic tools are recommended:

- Good quality sharp craft knife, with a selection of blades (see Fig. 18)
- Needle files (see Fig. 19)
- Fine drill bits: 0.5mm, 1mm and 2mm are the most commonly used sizes, but sets of drill bits from 0.3mm to 2mm are available relatively cheaply
- Pin vice or Archimedes' drill for use with the fine drill bits
- Steel straight edge (see Fig. 20)
- Small set square or similar
- Tweezers (see Fig. 21)

All of the above typically costs less than £20, the cost of a couple of kits, and is well worth the investment. If you can afford the additional expense, then the

PROS AND CONS OF MATERIAL TYPES

Material	Pros	Cons
Brass	• Excellent fine detail • Provides weight to improve running • More complicated detail easier to fabricate by etching than casting	• Difficult to modify • More complicated, higher skill levels required • Relatively more expensive • Can be more difficult to work
Plastic	• More forgiving of mistakes • Good for beginners • Relatively cheap • Good fine detail (on modern kits) • Easy to work/modify	• Level of detail sometimes limited; new kits excellent • Lightweight so requires ballasting to improve running
Resin	• Good level of detail • Cast in one piece for easier construction • Can be used by the modeller to cast limited run/bespoke components • Easier to modify than metals	• Lightweight model requires ballasting to improve running • Not as easy to work with as plastic
White metal	• Provides weight to the model for good running qualities	• On older kits/components the casting is poor and requires a lot of preparation and fettling • Prone to deformation
Wood	• Heavy material gives good running qualities • Realistic natural material • Can be relatively easily worked with the correct tools	• Limited level of detail possible at this scale • Not often used, limited supply of suitable good quality materials

purchase of a cutting mat I have found to be essential, especially if you have to share the kitchen table as a work bench. I use an A2-size mat, but mats are available in sizes from A5 to A0; it depends on what space you have available for working.

The A2 mat is big enough to lay out kit components so that you can work through dry runs and have space to set sections aside whilst working on something else; but at the end of the day it is down to personal preference and what space you have available in which to work.

SPECIALIST TOOLS

Beyond basic tool requirements, the following additional tools might be considered as investments and some will probably be essential when considering the construction of metal kits:

• Mini-drill with accessories such as cutting discs, grinding tips, drill bits (Rotacraft or similar), as shown in Fig. 22
• Engineer's square
• Scissors – several pairs for cutting paper, card and removing fine brass components from etches (see Fig. 23)

Fig. 18 Essential tools for the model maker include a good craft knife with a selection of blades and a scalpel blade for fine detail work.

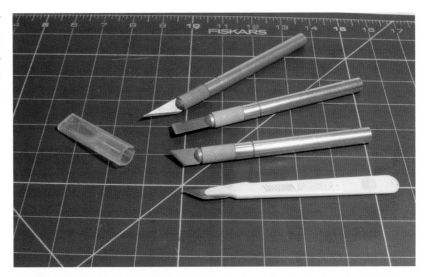

Fig. 19 Useful additions to the modeller's toolbox include a set of needle files in a range of shapes for fine adjustments; whilst for drilling holes, a box of fine drill bits (0.3mm to 1.6mm) used with either a pin vice or Archimedes' drill comes in handy.

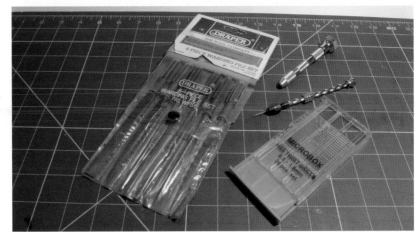

Fig. 20 To ensure accurate cutting and setting out, a steel rule/straight edge and a set square are required; the glass tile is ideal for a flat surface on which to set your parts.

Fig. 21   For placing parts, making fine adjustment or holding small items during painting and fixing, a selection of tweezers is invaluable.

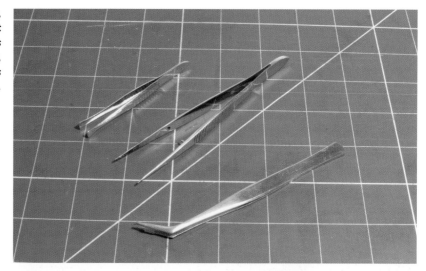

Fig. 22   A luxury item, but extremely useful if you can afford it, would be a boxed mini-drill and accessories, such as the Rotacraft one shown here.

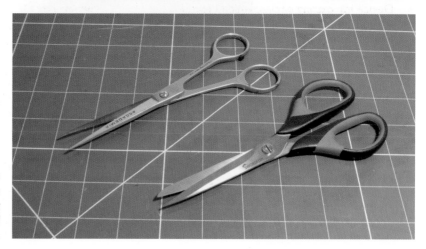

Fig. 23   It is useful to keep several pairs of sharp scissors in your toolbox for removing parts from brass etch and for cutting card.

Fig. 24   One of the more unusual tools available is this tool for marking and cutting circles, available cheaply from most good stationery suppliers.

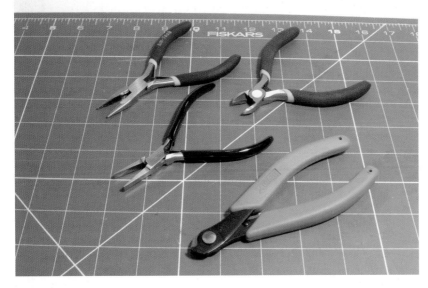

Fig. 25   A selection of pliers, side cutters and hard wire cutters are useful; and for brass kits, a pair of flat-faced pliers for bending and shaping brass components is essential.

- Scalpel blade for cutting out transfers and clear plastic glazing (*see* Fig. 18)
- Device for cutting circles, which I found in a card-making shop; this works on paper, card and thin plasticard and is very useful for scribing the curves for van end-walls when scratch building (*see* Fig. 24)
- Mini-vice for which I have built a small wooden stand and which is extremely useful when a 'second pair of hands' is required
- A good pair of mini-pliers and side-cutters (*see* Fig. 25)
- Square, flat-face pliers for folding brass parts (*see* Fig. 25)
- Set of small screwdrivers, both flat head and cross head

- Brass back-to-back OO wheel gauge for checking the metal wheel sets to ensure good running (*see* Fig. 26)
- Razor saw and selection of blades can be useful for cutting metals and plastic components (*see* Fig. 27)
- Glass-fibre stick
- Soldering iron – for use with brass kits, but also for more general electrical works on your model railway

A number of suppliers offer 'Modeller's Toolsets' that include much of the basic and more specialist tools in one box, as well as some other tools of perhaps less obvious necessity. These sets can be a good way of getting together most of the tools

Fig. 26 To check the wheels are to the correct gauge, a brass OO gauge back-to-back tool, such as the one here supplied by Mainly Trains, helps solve poor running rolling stock.

To ensure smooth running of the rolling stock that I make, whether from kits or scratch building, I make use of a brass back-to-back gauge to check all the wheel sets before installing them into the underframe. I have found that even RTR rolling stock can have back-to-back dimensions slightly 'off-gauge' straight out of the box, so the brass gauge comes in handy for checking these also. The brass gauge I use came from Mainly Trains (see Fig. 26), was relatively inexpensive at about £5, but has proved its value in resolving poor running problems with stock.

OTHER USEFUL BITS AND PIECES

As well as the list of tools I have provided, there are some things that can be utilized to help in the construction of kits that are not necessarily tools but which I have found can provide invaluable assistance in the construction of kits. The following items can be found around the house, or picked up cheaply from second-hand shops or market stalls:

- Glass tile – a machined piece of glass should be perfectly flat and is ideal for kit construction when assembling components that need to be kept absolutely square whilst the adhesive hardens off (see Fig. 20)
- Small off-cuts of timber, cut with 90-degree corners are also an excellent addition to your model-making toolbox – I make use of off-cuts of 2 × 1in timber and plywood of varying lengths for all sorts of uses including:

that you are likely to need at some point in one go, but the toolsets can be relatively expensive and it might be more sensible to buy the minimum basics first to see if kit building is what you want to do, before spending significant sums on tools that you will never, or only very occasionally, utilize.

I have built up my toolset over time, buying pieces as and when required, shopping around DIY stores for bargains, as well as antiques markets for old tools. I managed to pick up an engineer's square and a selection of screwdrivers from an antiques market, all in perfectly good working condition and for a fraction of the cost of buying them new.

Fig. 27 For the removal of parts from sprues or heavier duty cutting requirements, the use of a fine razor saw with a variety of blades and a cutting block could be of assistance.

- o   To support pieces of a kit during construction
- o   Wedge parts bits together whilst adhesive hardens
- o   Props for kits during construction whilst the adhesive is setting
- o   Weigh down items fixed together
- o   Protection of parts when using a clamp
- o   As a block to rest parts on when soldering
- Clothes pegs can serve the same purpose and are extremely useful when needing to hold parts together with pressure whilst the adhesive sets
- A selection of elastic bands is always handy, particularly for holding a van roof in place on the body whilst the adhesive sets to ensure that it binds and fixes squarely

FURTHER COMMENTS ON TOOLS

Sometimes I have been asked what has been the best investment in terms of tools and the answer is not necessarily the most expensive piece of equipment in your toolbox. For example, one of the most useful tools that I have bought in recent years was the device for marking and cutting circles. This cost the princely sum of £2 from an office supplies' shop, but has proved invaluable during the fabrication of parts for all sorts of modelling projects, not just rolling stock.

Another example of excellent value is the fine tweezers that I had for laboratory work whilst at university over twenty-five years ago. This cost very little to buy, but is extremely versatile with very fine-ribbed gripping points and magnetic for getting parts into, or retrieving lost parts from, difficult and fiddly locations when building kits.

In terms of what tools have proven to be of less value, probably the best example would be the side-cutters I originally bought for £2.99. Although these types of tools can be picked up cheaply, in my experience the cheaper pairs break easily and in the long run investing in slightly more expensive pairs (typically £5 to £10 each) is the better-value, long-term solution. The moral of the story is do not buy the cheapest – if you can afford something slightly more expensive, then it is worth spending the money once at a higher rate, than lots of cheap items replaced much more frequently and ultimately costing more money.

For the more specialist tools, the most useful and value-for-money item that I have been lucky enough to get as a Christmas present was the Rotacraft tool (see Fig. 22). The particular model I have cost about £40, but came with many accessories, including grinding bits, sanding bits, drills and polishing tools. This all comes in a ready-made toolbox for storage and, as I have been able to demonstrate on numerous occasions, has many uses around the home, other than the model railway, and I would recommend adding this to your Christmas list!

Fig. 28   One of the most useful and cheapest aids for the modeller is a selection of wooden blocks. These have many and varied uses, including for those times when you need to prop parts of a kit together whilst the adhesive sets.

CHAPTER THREE

BUILDING A WAGON KIT

INTRODUCTION

In Chapter 2, I provided a summary overview of the types of kits available today and the relative merits of each type of kit in terms of material types, degree of accuracy and limitations. In this chapter I will cover the construction of wagon and van kits as a prelude to kit conversions and scratch building rolling stock, which I will cover in more detail later. I also provide a brief overview of the range of kits on offer and specifically consider the varying skill levels required to complete them.

I have used worked examples to show the techniques and issues that a modeller should bear in mind when constructing different types of kits – from basic to specialized.

Before looking at the way these kits are put together, it is useful to cover some basic principles that apply no matter how simple, or complicated, the kit.

STARTING WITH THE INSTRUCTIONS

The most important part of building any kit is to read the instructions all the way through before starting anything. This will help you to get a picture in your mind of how the wagon or van is going to materialize from the collection of parts sitting in front of you on the workbench or table, as shown in Figs 29 and 30. In the case of most, but not all, models there will also be a series of sketches or drawings provided with the kit, illustrating the key stages of the construction process, showing how and where parts fit together. This, unfortunately, is not always to the same standard and on some kits you may only get a list of instructions, or construction steps, whilst sometimes you may be lucky and get an exploded diagram of part or all of the model and a picture of what the finished article should look like when you have toiled away at it for a few hours or days. In these circumstances, photographs of the prototype

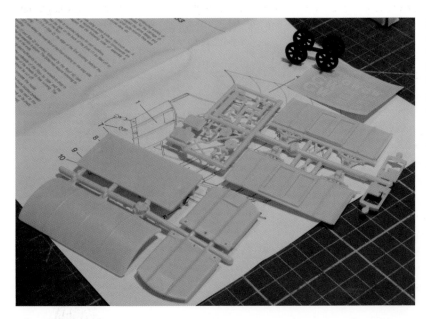

Fig. 29 Laying out the parts of the model on the workbench before you start building enables you to look through the instructions and familiarize yourself with all the parts.

Fig. 30   In the case of the Airfix Models BR Mineral open wagon kit, the instructions provided are clear and easy to understand.

are even more important; the photographs will help to clarify what needs to go where on the model, especially if the model is of a prototype where there may have been numerous changes or adaptations over the operating life.

Some kits are provided with only a very limited set of instructions and possibly an exploded diagram, from which the modeller is supposed to build the kit. These types of kits in the main are aimed at the more experienced modeller, who will probably have a good idea of what the wagon or van is going to look like before starting the model kit.

FIRST STEPS

Dry runs of some stages of the kit construction are a useful exercise in not just giving you an understanding of how things fit together before you fix them permanently, but also it is a way of checking that you have all the appropriate parts and that nothing is missing. There is nothing more infuriating when modelling than working through a kit only to get stumped when you cannot find the next piece because it has been mislaid or even lost.

As a tip, I always keep all the pieces for any kit that I am working on either in a re-sealable bag or plastic box with a lid, to ensure that nothing gets lost. The box can also be used to collect together all

the additional detailing parts that I will need for the wagon or van, before starting to build the kit, again to make sure that I do not need to order or buy something part way through a project. This I find is a good way of checking I have everything and a good way of stock-taking components that I can then replenish in good time before starting something new.

As with most things in life, the quality of the product, i.e. the finished kit, is directly proportional to the amount of time that you spend making it. If you rush through the kit, sticking things together, without cleaning off joints or checking with dry runs to ensure that they fit together correctly, or not waiting until joints have hardened off, for example, you will likely end up with a van or wagon that will not look right, invariably will not run smoothly and, worst of all, may end up breaking or falling apart and need re-building. This could result in the kit being completely ruined, which would be a waste of time, effort and money if you have to scrap something and start all over again. In these times of austerity, I am sure that unless you are financially flush with funds for your hobby, having to 'buy that expensive kit again' won't go down well with the domestic financial director.

The trick is to learn to be patient. I have been guilty of rushing things in the past and learnt the subsequent lessons; I now try to be patient and leave things to harden off or dry for several days between key stages of the construction process. Some of this is driven by the need to carry out other things around the home or even work (!), but the results are obvious to me in the production of better models, which I hope you will agree from the photographs of the rolling stock that I have made that have been included in this book.

PREPARATORY WORK

As part of the process of building a kit, you also need to think before you start about how you are going to finish it off with painting and decals, and to a lesser degree, where preferred, the application of weathering. During the construction process, or even before, it is often better and easier to paint all, or at least some, sections or key parts before fixing together; whilst for other parts it is better to paint after construction has been completed; for example, the overall body after you have formed the corner joints.

Preparing kits or parts of kits before construction is also a vital part of the kit building process. Fettling, as it is often referred to, is the process of cleaning away any flash or imperfections in the kit parts that

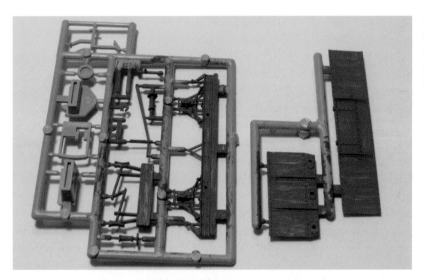

Fig. 31 It is often helpful to pre-paint some or all of the parts of kit prior to removal from the sprues for construction.

Fig. 32 After removing the parts from the sprues using a craft knife, razor saw or side cutters, fine filing adjustments to parts should be carefully undertaken with a fine file.

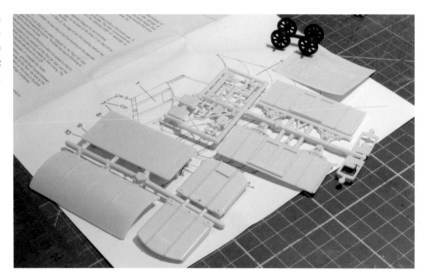

Fig. 33 Example of a Ratio van kit parts and instruction sheet removed from the packaging and laid out for inspection.

may have been produced during the kit moulding process. This only really applies to kits or parts made from white metal, plastic or resin that have been cast or moulded. Brass kits tend to be etched frets, with only minor cleaning up of the burrs where parts are removed from the fret required as part of the preparation process.

It is important also to bear in mind that as a result of the casting process for white metal and etching of brass, the metal will need cleaning and de-greasing to get rid of the compounds used in the production process that coat the metal, before priming and painting the metal parts.

CONSTRUCTING A BASIC KIT

To provide some guidance and advice on the construction of straightforward or simple rolling stock kits, I will describe the process from opening the box to completing the decals and running on the layout. Along the way I will explain how to overcome common problems and will provide tips to help the beginner through the process. For the basis of this exercise, I have assumed a complete beginner is approaching the construction of a piece of rolling stock for the first time.

In Chapter 2, I went through the process of identifying what tools might be needed, and in the earlier part of this chapter I discussed some of the preparatory activities that are required before starting to build a kit; now it is time to have a go at building something.

BUILDING A VAN KIT

For the purposes of this example, I chose an old Ratio Iron Mink kit (Ratio ref: 5063, newer models Ratio ref: 563) that I had in my box of kits waiting to be made. The first part of the process is to open the box containing the kit and carefully remove the parts, some if not all of which may be attached to sprues, and lay the parts on the working surface. For the Iron Mink kit, it is apparent at first glance that this kit comprises six main parts, plus some detail components and a set of plastic wheels.

The instructions are typical of this type of kit, comprising a single-sided sheet with written instructions and an exploded diagram of how all the parts go together. To provide further information as to what the finished wagon should look like, reference to a photograph of the prototype would be useful and for those looking at Great Western railway wagons, the invaluable reference sources provided by Russell (1971) and Atkins *et al.* (2013) are highly recommended.

After reading all of the instructions and reviewing the drawing, the first step is to remove the parts in the sequence suggested in the assembly instructions. As a tip, do not remove smaller parts

Fig. 34   When removing parts from the sprue, it is recommended that the parts be supported using one of the blocks of wood that you have collected for your model making.

Fig. 35   Cleaning up the cut marks and removing unwanted materials from the moulding process, referred to as flash, can be completed with needle files.

from the sprues until required for assembly, as they are likely to get lost or broken. For this type of kit, painting can easily be left until the kit has been constructed, as there are no difficult-to-access parts or fine detail parts requiring pre-construction painting.

When removing the parts from the moulding sprues, it is advisable to use a sharp craft knife and support the part and sprue connection on a piece of wood to prevent damage to, or deformation of, the part during removal, as shown in Fig. 34. Alternatively it is possible to use specialist sprue cutters. However, in either case, the use of fine files will be necessary

to remove flash and unwanted material at the sprue connection, as shown in Fig. 35.

When using files to tidy up the parts, do this carefully and a small bit at a time to avoid damage. It is also helpful to check the part against the photographs of the prototype to ensure that the model will look correct, whilst you are carrying out the fettling. When you are happy with the fettling of the parts, do a dry run of the assembly stage to check that the parts fit together correctly. If necessary carry out further fine adjustments with fine files or glass paper, again going through this process a small bit at a time to avoid damaging the model.

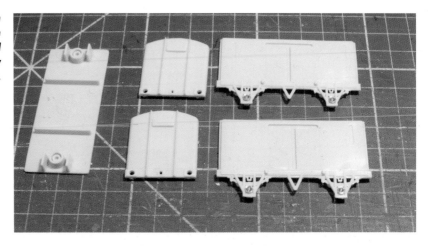

Fig. 36   All the main parts have been removed and prepared for dry run assembly before construction.

After the dry run of one end and one sidewall, it will be necessary to check that the floor fits correctly before the side and end walls are fixed together. In the case of the Iron Mink van kit, the instructions indicate that the moulding pips on the inside face of the walls need to be filed flat, to ensure a snug fit of the floor with the end wall. This needs to be done before fixing any of the parts together.

At this stage you also need to decide whether you plan to use the buffers and coupling hook details for the buffer beam as supplied in the kit, or whether you want to replace them with alternative detail parts. In Chapter 4, we will look at using alternative components to details of wagons and vans, and the installation of these will be discussed further there. Assuming that you wish to proceed with the buffers and coupling hook as supplied in the kit, these parts need to be carefully removed from the sprue and inserted into the holes provided on the buffer beam, which is integral to the end walls on this kit.

The buffers and coupling hooks are small and extremely fragile parts that can easily be damaged or lost when removing from the sprue. To do this carefully I find the best solution is to support the sprue and part on a piece of wood and whilst cutting the part free, place one of your fingers on the part to gently hold it in place so that it does not twist, break or fly off to disappear somewhere on the floor.

Checking the fit of the buffers and coupling hook in the pre-drilled holes in the buffer beams is carried out before fixing permanently with drops of liquid

polystyrene cement. When the parts have set, the kit can then be constructed following the steps and drawings in the assembly instructions for guidance. To get the best results do not rush, and use liquid polystyrene cement applied either with the fine needle applicator or a brush. Using small spots of adhesive, bring the joints together and check to ensure that the joint is square, then apply a further thin stream of adhesive to the inside of the joint to strengthen and reinforce the joint.

This particular kit goes together easily and quickly after all the preparatory work I have described and the final shape of the wagon soon becomes apparent. When both sides of the wagon have been fixed together, it is advisable to check that it is square by using a flat glass tile on which to sit the model. At this stage it is also a good idea to spring open the axle boxes and drop in the wheel sets to check alignment and that the wheels are running freely in the axle boxes. Set the model aside to dry if all is well.

Whilst the body of the kit is drying, take the roof and remove from the sprue. The edges of the roof will require fine fettling with glass paper and fine files to remove flash and to ensure that it is ready to fix to the body.

The brake gear and brake lever can be removed from the sprue and checked for fitting to the model. The brake gear on the Iron Mink van only fits on one side, indicated by the locating pips on the underside of the wagon floor. With the wheels in place, check the fit of the brake gear and adjust as necessary with

Fig. 37   When the sole bars have been fixed to the body, the wheels should be installed to check accuracy and that they are free-running.

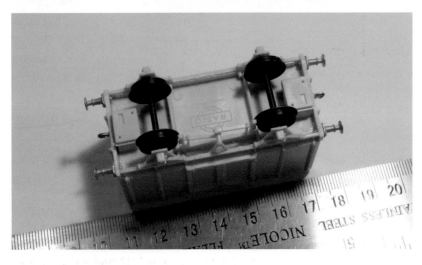

Fig. 38   Underside view of the van kit during construction to show the addition of brake gear, which is carefully aligned to ensure that the brake shoes are in line with the wheel treads.

a fine file to ensure a snug fit. It is important that the brake shoes are in line with the wheel treads, but do not impede the free movement of the wheels, as shown in Fig. 38. When you are happy with the fit, fix in place with adhesive. Reference to prototype photographs comes in useful at this point, as the fitting of brake gear to many wagons and vans varies considerably, with similar vehicles fitted with brake gear on one or both sides.

The brake lever fits at one end to the 'V' hanger on the sole bar and at the other end to the sole bar above the axle box. A trial run shows that these fixing points require the lever to arch between the two points. This lever is a fine detail part that can easily break, so to fix this without breaking I recommend that you first glue the joint and fix to the 'V' hanger and let it harden off for a couple of hours. Once dried, apply a spot of glue to the sole bar fixing point and gently push the lever into position; hold in place by hand or with a weight and let the glue harden off before removing.

To provide some additional ballast to the model, fix a steel weight to the floor inside the van. The weight should be placed centrally on the floor and held in place with contact adhesive. The amount of ballast to be added is down to personal preference, but I like to add some to all wagons and vans that I build, as it improves the track adhesion and thus the running qualities of the finished model. Do not overdo the ballast, as your locomotive might begin to struggle with a train load of heavily ballasted wagons to move.

The type of coupling to be used also depends on your personal preference. The tension lock coupling supplied with the kit is quite large. It is perfectly possible to use three-link couplings, utilizing the hole for the dummy coupling hook. I use tension lock couplings on my layout, so I complete the kit accordingly, except that I replace the supplied coupling with

a smaller Bachmann mini-coupling (Bachmann ref: 36-025) as this is less obtrusive.

Once all the body has dried, and before fixing the roof, the body and underframe can be painted all over GWR freight wagon grey, as shown in Fig. 39. Wheel sets should be removed during painting and it is important to take care not to get any paint in the axle box bearings, as this will affect the smooth running of the wheels. The roof should be painted white if representing a newly out-shopped wagon, or can be painted white then weathered grey to represent a wagon that has been in service. When the paint is dry the roof can be fixed to the body,

Fig. 39   On completion of the assembly, the body work has been painted in the appropriate railway company colours and the roof placed loosely on the body to check alignment and fitting.

Fig. 40   When the painting has been completed and allowed to dry, the final detail to be added to bring the kit alive as a piece of model rolling stock is the addition of decals and couplings.

Fig. 41 The completed Ratio kit of the GWR Iron Mink van makes a nice addition to the rolling stock fleet.

although I tend to fix the roof and body together after I have applied the decals, as it makes it easier to hold the wagon before the roof is fixed in place.

The completed model is now ready-to-run on your layout. This type of kit can be built and finished quite quickly: typically, after preparation, all the fixing and modifying can be completed in a couple of hours, with painting and decals application to finish. However, do not rush; let the adhesives dry thoroughly for at least twenty-four hours before starting any of the painting. Let the paint dry (two coats may be required) at least twenty-four hours between coats before adding the decals. The result is a nice, well-built, neat model, which will look good on your layout and which you know you have built, rather than just lifted it out of a box – a very satisfying feeling.

CONSTRUCTING AN OPEN WAGON KIT

Constructing a basic open wagon kit is not too dissimilar to the method for a van kit, as described in the previous section, except that there is a need to paint the inside of the completed model and that you need to be aware that mistakes made during construction cannot be hidden under a roof! In addition, you will probably need to consider fabricating a load for the wagon, unless you wish to run it empty.

For this example, I used a Cooper Craft coal wagon (Cooper Craft ref: 1002), to which I added metal fine-scale wheels (Gibson 12mm diameter, eight-spoke) with brass bearings and white metal buffers (ABS) to the correct GWR pattern, and I replaced the tension lock couplings supplied with the kit with Bachmann mini-type (ref: 36-025).

This type of kit benefits from painting most of the parts before cutting from the sprues, so a coat of GWR wagon grey was duly applied to the parts required, checking against the instructions for the correct parts needed to complete the kit. The alternate and spare parts not required for the kit were carefully removed from the sprues and transferred to my stock of parts kept in my spares' box for future use in scratch building or kit conversions.

The kit is then constructed following the instructions as supplied, which comprise a list of logical steps for construction and exploded parts' drawings to show the relationship between the various parts for those not familiar with this type of wagon kit. Starting with the underframe, the first step is to install brass bearings to the axle boxes and fix in place with a spot of super glue, as described in more detail in Chapter 4, whilst the sole bars were still attached to the sprues.

To ensure good running qualities and no wobbling of the finished wagon, I fixed the sole bars to

Fig. 42   The basic parts of a simple open wagon kit, such as the Cooper Craft coal wagon kit, with some of the parts painted before removal from the sprue.

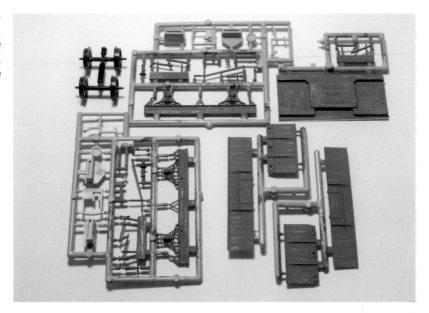

the underside of the wagon floor and then dropped in the wheel sets to check alignment of axle boxes and that all was square and the wheels were free-running. It is best to then leave the wagon overnight to allow the glue to harden off. I tend to use a glass plate to put the wagon on, wedged between two blocks of wood, to ensure that the axles remain square to the body and wheel sets.

Whilst waiting for the underframe to harden off, the next step is to prepare the white metal buffers. Using a 2mm diameter drill bit, first bore out the pre-drilled holes in the buffer beam by gently twisting a pin vice with the drill bit clamped in place. The shaft of the buffers to go into the holes in the buffer beam will probably need fine adjustment with a needle file to ensure a snug push fit through the holes. Do not force the buffers through the holes as this will stress the plastic and could lead to the buffer beam distorting or even breaking.

When you are happy with the fit of the buffers, these are inserted and a spot of contact adhesive (for example, UHU) is used on the rear face of the buffer beam to hold them in place. A coupling hook can also be inserted and fixed at the same time, either the plastic one supplied with the kit or a replacement white metal component. The wagon ends can then be left to harden off overnight.

The next step is to add brake gear and Dean Churchward (DC) brake handles to the underframe before adding the wagon body, starting at one end and working around the wagon one side at a time, as shown in Fig. 43. I found that to ensure a flush fit of the end walls of the wagon to the underframe, it was necessary to remove any excess buffer shank protruding from the rear face of the buffer beam. To do this, I carefully trimmed the shanks using a side cutter (white metal is soft and easily cut), followed by the use of fine files to smooth the cut surface.

Liquid polystyrene cement is used to fix all of the plastic kit components together and is applied sparingly using the needle applicator on the glue pot or with a small brush.

When the body is square at the corners, it is then left to harden off upside down on a glass tile to ensure a square flat top surface to the wagon sides. When dry, use fine files and fine-grade glass paper to round off the wagon corners between the top edge and the lower edge rivet strip detail to match the profile of the prototype, as shown in Fig. 44.

Rounding off the corners should be carried out gently and a small bit at time, checking regularly to see that the corner remains vertical and square at the inner joint edges. Use a photograph of the

Fig. 43 After removing and cleaning up the parts, bodywork construction commences with the underframe and then addition of the wagon ends and sides.

Fig. 44 To improve the look of the finished model use a flat-face file to round off the body corners to match the prototype.

Fig. 45 Final painting of the wagon prior to application of decals and the trial fit of a false floor for the wagon load, described further in Chapter 4.

prototype to compare what the final shape should look like. Do not attack the model as though you are grinding down the edge of a door, otherwise the wagon will end up with misshaped corners or, worse still, too much of the plastic body will be removed and you will end up with a hole!

When satisfied with the shape of the corners, apply a second coat of GWR wagon grey paint and pick out the brake handles in white, as shown in Fig. 45. You will also note that in Fig. 45 I have begun the process of adding a false floor and load, as described in Chapter 4 and shown in Figs 110–114.

Transfers were Pressfix from the HMRS range, as I prefer these to the waterslide decals provided with the kit (see Fig. 115). As the wagon is open, you have the choice as to whether you wish to add a load or run it empty. I chose to add a load of coal for use on my layout and constructed a load as described in Chapter 4.

CONSTRUCTING PRE-PRINTED KITS

Another type of kit, although less common these days, is the pre-printed wagon kit, where the decals have been printed on to a pre-painted or coloured plastic body. All the modeller needs to do is carefully cut the parts from the sprues and fix together. A couple of examples are included in this section (an open wagon, van and tank wagon) for reference, to show how these types of kits are put together and, more importantly, to provide a few tips for the modeller when working with these types of kits.

The quality of the kits and moulding is very good. The key issues with these types of kits are the careful removal of the parts and the sparing use of glue to fix them together to avoid spoiling the coloured body parts and pre-printed decals. All the examples that are included here make up into nice well-detailed wagons, although the Slater's open wagon and Ratio van are unfortunately both discontinued items at the time of writing. The examples used here were obtained from eBay for reasonable prices of approximately £10 per kit including postage.

CONSTRUCTION OF A PRE-PRINTED VAN KIT

The Ratio pre-printed kit for the Harvey's Bristol Cream van is a relatively old kit, but it is possible to occasionally pick up unmade examples of the kit at sales, swap meets or from on-line auctions. This van kit included metal wheels and brass bearings.

Construction of the van kit is relatively simple and straightforward. The instructions provided are clear

Fig. 46   The Ratio Models pre-printed Harvey's Bristol Cream van kit as removed from the box to study before construction.

and concise, and when combined with the exploded parts' drawing provide a reasonably comprehensive set of instructions for putting the kit together. As discussed earlier, it is important to read the instructions fully before starting and to familiarize yourself with the parts and, with the aid of the exploded drawing, to visualize how the kit will go together before starting anything.

I found that to install the brass bearings in the axle boxes it was necessary to drill out the boxes with a 2mm diameter bit, to ensure that when inserted, the flange on the bearing fitted flush with the inside face of the axle box. To drill out the axle boxes, take a 2mm drill bit and, using a pin vice or Archimedes' fine drill, twist the bit by hand to remove a small bit at a time, being careful to check that the drill bit does not go too far into the axle box.

After checking to ensure the correct depth, I then used a spot of cyanoacrylate (super glue) in each axle box and pressed home the brass bearings using the flat end of my tweezers or a small screwdriver to get a flush fit, being careful not to damage the bearing. All of this work on the fitting of bearings is accomplished either before removing the sole bars from the sprue or after removing them but before commencing construction of the underframe.

Following the instructions provided, the underframe is constructed first by fixing the sole bars on to

Fig. 47   The kit is best started with the completion of the underframe construction before adding the bodywork.

each side of the main floor component, as shown in Fig. 47. This was placed with the upper floor surface down on to a glass tile to ensure that it stayed flat and then the wheel sets were installed to check all was square, i.e. that the axles were perpendicular to the floor edges and the wheels were free-running in the bearings. I use a small block of wood each side of the underframe to keep it all square whilst the adhesive is drying and I leave the wheels in place

Fig. 48   With pre-coloured body parts, removal of the parts from the sprue and cleaning up needs to be carefully carried out to prevent damage to the outer finished surface.

Fig. 49   The fine detail parts to add to the kit are also pre-coloured and when fixing care should be taken not to over-apply the adhesive.

whilst the glue hardens off to ensure that it remains square. Put this to one side and leave overnight to dry to get the best results.

Whilst the underframe was drying, I removed the body parts and cleaned up the flash from the moulding process as preparation for the next stage of construction. When the underframe has hardened off, the next stage was to add the detailing parts, starting with the brake gear, then the vacuum cylinder and then the brake lever.

The kit as supplied has axle box tie bars moulded in place, which need to be removed according to the instructions. If the tie bars are carefully cut flush with the axle box at each end, you will be left with two pieces of thin plastic rod – I use this to form the link bars between the two sets of brake gear. This is not part of the instructions, but a way of adding a bit more detail to your wagon kit, a subject covered in more detail in the next chapter.

Once finished with the brake gear and connecting rods, the next stage was to fit the coupling of choice. The mounting blocks supplied with the kit for the tension lock coupler were cut from the sprue for use with my preferred choice of coupling, the Bachmann mini-type, although other types and methods of coupling can be considered and it is at this stage, before

commencing the construction further, that the modeller needs to check and fit their preferred coupling arrangement.

Before constructing the body of the van, I fixed the buffers and cosmetic coupling hooks to each buffer beam that forms part of the end wall mouldings. It is easier to fit these components with the end wall lying flat on the work surface, rather than when the body has been fixed together. It is often necessary to ream out the holes for the buffers and the coupling hook, all of which is less fiddly and easier to undertake prior to construction. Once happy that the buffers and hooks are fitted squarely, these can be left for the glue to harden off.

The body was constructed around the floor/underframe sub-assembly, starting with one end wall and one sidewall. When satisfied that these walls are squarely joined and fixed, the second sidewall and end wall can be added to form the whole box of the body. The upright vacuum pipes shown fitted to the wagon should be added after the body has been fixed together, as they will easily get knocked off or damaged if added before fixing the body together.

The ventilators were cut from the sprue and carefully pushed through the pre-drilled holes in the roof, before fixing with a spot of glue on the underside of the roof. Fixing the ventilators in this way avoids any unsightly glue build-up on the top surface of the roof. When dry, the roof and ventilators were painted matt white and left to dry before fixing the roof to the body. If preferred the underframe could be painted matt black and the brake lever handle picked out in white.

CONSTRUCTION OF A PRE-PRINTED TANK WAGON

The PECO tank wagon kit is one of four types of tank wagon that can still be picked up for around £10 to £12 (at the time of writing) and the Royal Daylight fuel tank wagon illustrated here makes an extremely neat and well-modelled item. I have used another version of the tank wagon kit, the United Dairies milk tank, as the basis for a conversion project, to create a representation of a GWR milk tank wagon, as described further in Chapter 5.

Fig. 50   The completed model when carefully put together is difficult to distinguish from RTR items and makes a colourful addition to your PO wagon fleet.

The PECO tank wagon kits are weighted with metal weights inside the tank body and make up, with care, into a model that runs extremely well on the plastic (Hardlon) wheels provided, which if preferred could be replaced by metal wheel sets.

The PECO Royal Daylight tank wagon kits come in a box with the main tank already preformed, painted and lettered and displayed in the window on the box lid. Opening the box reveals a tray of parts and a comprehensive instruction sheet, with both written instructions and a step-by-step picture guide.

The kits comprise relatively few parts (see Fig. 52) to be fixed together and a finished model can be accomplished in a relatively short period of time. The one important point to bear in mind with this type of kit is the choice of adhesive to use to fix the parts together. The varied types of plastic used in the kit construction necessitate the use of a super glue type adhesive; standard polystyrene cement will not fix some of the material types together.

The instructions are clear and easy to follow; the only additional advice would be to make sure that you do a dry run of each section, so that you understand what the final piece will look like before fixing permanently with the super glue.

Adding additional or extra detail to the model is for preference; I chose to model the kit as per the instructions and did not add any additional detail components, except for adding the connecting bar between the two sets of brake gear on each side of the wagon, using an off-cut of the thicker gauge wire supplied with the kit for use as tension rods. For the purposes of this example, I also chose to use the Hardlon wheels supplied with the kit, running in the PECO plastic bearings, as these proved to run extremely well.

Once the chassis was completed, I opted to paint all of the underframe matt black to hide glue marks, areas where fine adjustments had been made using a file and to take the 'plastic look' off the finished model.

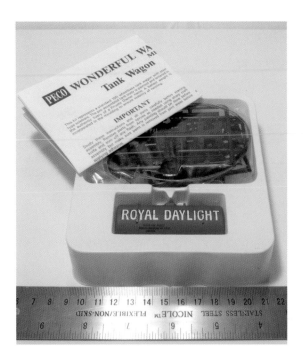

Fig. 51 The PECO Wonderful Wagon tank wagon kits come in a protective tray that can be used as your temporary storage for parts during the assembly process.

Fig. 52 The pre-formed and painted tank in its finished livery and decals; chassis parts in one bag, metal 'W' irons in another, and wheels and bearings in another.

Fig. 53 The construction of the model can be quickly and easily accomplished and the completed model looks good on the layout.

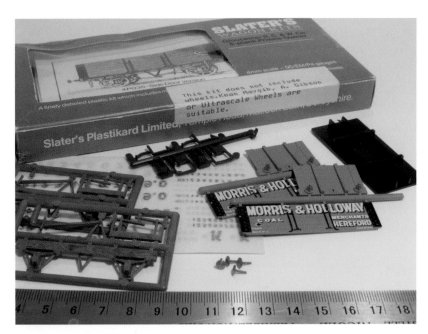

Fig. 54 An example of a pre-printed open wagon is one of the many formerly produced by Slater's Plastikard, such as this example of a coal wagon kit representing a Morris and Holloway of Hereford prototype.

CONSTRUCTING A PRE-PRINTED OPEN WAGON

The Slater's pre-printed open wagon, used as an example here, is currently not available as a new kit, but unbuilt examples of this particular model, and many more similar wagons, can still be picked up at swap meets, fairs or via on-line auctions for reasonable prices around the £10 mark. This particular example is the 'Morris and Holloway', Coal Merchants of Hereford wagon with a grey overall body, ironwork picked out in black, black underframe and white shaded-black lettering.

The Slater's pre-printed open wagon kits do not come with wheels and bearings, so it is up to the modeller to supply metal wheels and bearings from another source. In this case I opted to use Gibson 12mm diameter open-spoke wheels and brass bearings.

The ends and sides were carefully removed from the sprues and, following the instructions, one end and one sidewall were fixed together after cleaning up the sprue mould points and mitre joints at the corners. I made use of my glass tile here to check that the joint was square and the top edges were flat when joined. I also used a small 90-degree set square

to check that the joint was a right angle. This process was repeated for the other end wall and sidewall and then both sub-assemblies were left to harden off before proceeding.

As the sides of the wagon body are pre-printed, it is essential to be sparing with the application of liquid adhesive to the mitre joints, to prevent surplus glue squeezing out of the joint during fixing, on to the pre-coloured and lettered surfaces. I found that the use of 'Revell Contacta Professional' with application of the liquid cement via a fine needle applicator to be extremely useful in these circumstances. The trick is to apply a small amount, even a few drops, sufficient for the joint to hold and then go over the inside of the joint with a fine stream of liquid cement to strengthen the join.

Whilst the body sections were hardening, I took the opportunity to paint the underframe and ironwork detail on the sole bar matt black using a fine brush. The painted parts were left to dry for twenty-four hours before proceeding further. Construction of the kit then progressed following the instructions provided. The body side sub-assemblies were fixed together before dropping the floor in to place. The only change from the instructions that I made to the

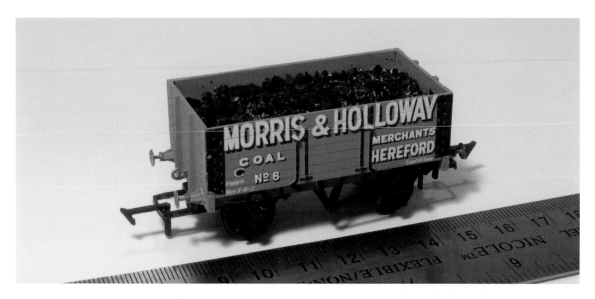

Fig. 55   The completed model ready-to-run requires very little additional painting and the addition of a coal load adds to the realism of the model.

kit was that I chose to replace the plastic coupling hooks with white metal components.

On completion of the wagon, I opted to fit a permanent coal load to the wagon, using the technique described in Chapter 4, and added a makers' plate and wagon running number using Pressfix decals.

CONSTRUCTING MORE COMPLICATED KITS

The construction of more complicated wagon kits should not be seen as something for the more advanced modeller. The kits produced by the likes of Parkside Dundas, 51L, Cambrian Models and others, as well as in the past by the likes of Colin Ashby, Ian Kirk, Falcon Brassworks and others, only differ from the more straightforward kits by the number of parts required, the inclusion of more detailed parts requiring sub-assembly before construction of the overall kit and the requirement on the part of the modeller to provide paint, couplings, wheels and decals of choice.

CONSTRUCTING MORE COMPLICATED PLASTIC KITS

The construction of these types of plastic kits is very similar to the construction of the more basic kit, except that there is usually much more detail and sub-assembly work required to complete the overall model. Good examples of the more complicated plastic kits are the ones supplied by Parkside Dundas, of which I have built a fair number over the years, as well as using some of their kits as the basis for conversions, as shown in Chapter 5.

Typically these kits comprise much more choice in terms of components that can be used to create different versions of the prototype and therefore it is essential that when looking to start on one of these types of kits you carry out your research and try and get a picture or two of the completed prototype to which you can refer.

As examples of this type of kit, I have included some images of completed models from the Parkside Dundas range that I currently have operating on my layout, some of which were built over thirty years ago but which are still going strong. Of these kits the most complex, or perhaps most fiddly to get right, is probably the Bloater wagon with all the external

Fig. 56   The Parkside GWR Mink D and Mink G van kits are more detailed and require the modeller to provide decals.

Fig. 57   The additional fine detail evident on the Parkside Bloater kit requires a steady hand and patience, but the finished model is worth the effort.

additional detail that can be added, as shown in Fig. 57.

The key lesson that I learned when building these kits was that it is important to take your time and not to rush during the construction process. To watch the completed model, nicely detailed and painted, running on your layout is extremely satisfying and justification for the time spent putting it together.

In Chapter 4, I have included a step-by-step guide to building and detailing a more complicated kit.

CONSTRUCTION OF A WHITE METAL WAGON KIT

To show the techniques used for the construction of a white metal kit, a 51L white metal kit of a Cambrian Railway open wagon has been used as

Fig. 58 The 51L white-metal kit of a Cambrian Railway's slate wagon provides a simple open wagon kit of an unusual prototype.

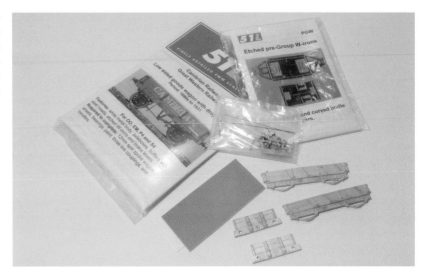

Fig. 59 The kit comprises a selection of brass and white-metal components, as well as plasticard for the floor, requiring the modeller to use a number of different adhesives to complete the model.

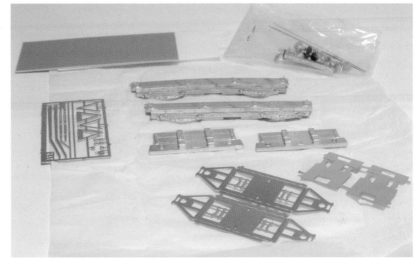

a worked example. The kit as supplied comprises a number of white metal parts, two pieces of plasticard and two brass frets. The white metal parts form the main body, as well as the detail components for the brake gear and buffers. One of the two pieces of plasticard is embossed to represent wooden planks for the wagon floor, whilst the second, thinner sheet of plasticard is intended as packing material below the floor.

The first of the two brass frets supplied has etched parts for the brake lever and 'V' hangers. The second brass fret is for the 'W' irons and supporting frames

to build either a rigid or a compensated (rocking) chassis, as shown in Fig. 59. Starting with the brass fret, the 'W' irons were removed with a sharp pair of fine scissors and the parts fold up along the half-etch lines. A tip here is to apply a thin stream of solder or adhesive to the inside of the fold line to reinforce the part.

Using a 2mm diameter drill bit ream out the holes in the 'W' irons for the brass axle bearings. This may also require the use of a fine, round broach or file to open out the hole to accept the bearing. Insert the bearings, being sure to insert them the correct way

Fig. 60   The first part of the model to make up is the etched brass compensation units; these are folded up and the wheels test-fitted.

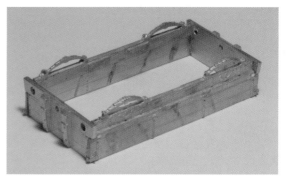

Fig. 61   The white metal bodywork is fixed utilizing a flat glass tile surface to ensure it remains square until set.

round, and push so that they are flush with the internal face of the 'W' iron. Take the white metal axle box castings and carefully ream out the holes that go over the brass bearing. The white metal components are soft, so any reaming needs to be carried out a small amount at a time to avoid any risk of damage to the part.

When satisfied with the fit, the white metal part should sit over the brass bearing and flush with the external face of the 'W' iron. This can then be held in place by streaming a small amount of super glue around the join using a fine piece of wire. Leave to set, then spring the 'W' irons apart gently and drop in the wheel sets to check that they are free-running. Next, fold up the brass base plate and test fit to the 'W' iron sub-assembly. The plates can be folded up to make either a rigid or rocking chassis; the choice is down to the modeller. When completed, set aside these elements of the kit and start on the body.

The main wagon body comprises four white metal parts, with the sole bars and springs forming part of the sidewall castings. Clean off the flash from the moulding process and then take one end and one side and fix together. Use a flat glass tile to ensure that the parts are level and check that the corner is 90 degrees. Whilst these parts are setting, repeat the process for the second end and sidewalls. Leave both sub-assemblies to dry for at least a couple of hours, then fix together and check to ensure it is square, then leave overnight to harden off.

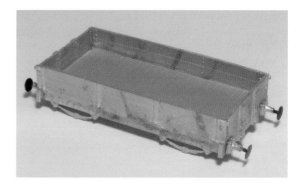

Fig. 62   The plasticard sub-floor and floor sections are inserted from above into the body and fixed securely in place with impact adhesive.

Measure the internal dimensions of the wagon body and cut the floor and sub-floor to size. Bore out the holes for buffers and coupling hooks, and fix in place. Install the floors as described in the instructions and as shown in Fig. 62. Place the folded-up 'W' irons on the underside of the floor to check the height relative to the springs. On the example that I constructed, I needed to add 1mm of plasticard packing to raise the level of the 'W' irons. When satisfied, fix in place and check running qualities.

When the 'W' irons are fixed, install the 'V' hangers on the internal and external face of the sole bar. Prior to placement, the 'V' hanger should be bored out with a 0.5mm drill to allow insertion of a connecting rod formed from brass wire, as shown

Fig. 63   Assembly of etched brass 'V' hanger and brake lever can be undertaken whilst the body is hardening off.

Fig. 64   The compensation units should be fixed to the floor and, where necessary, plasticard packing added to ensure that the wheels are aligned with axle box springs.

in Fig. 63. The white metal brake gear will also need to have the central crank opened out with the same drill bit. To ensure all of the pieces of the brake gear are aligned, first fix the brake gear in place between the wheels, ensuring alignment with the wheel treads (see Fig. 64). I found it was necessary to use a scrap piece of plasticard to provide support to the brake gear.

Next thread the brass wire through the brake gear and then thread the brass internal and external 'V' hangers on to the same piece of wire, using 0.5mm wire as a jig to check alignment. Fix in place with a spot of super glue, fixing the external 'V' hanger in place last. I found the external 'V' hanger needed to be trimmed to the correct length – check with a trial fit before fixing in place. Use a piece of the 0.5mm wire at least 20mm long to ensure it extends well beyond the 'V' hanger and brake gear. Fold up the brake lever and ratchet from the etch parts; fix the lever in place threaded on to the 0.5mm wire and hold in place with a spot of super glue. When hardened, trim the wire with side cutters.

The plasticard floor for the kit is embossed to represent planking and is supplied in a brown colour. I used the GWR wagon grey as a thin wash coat over the floor to let some of the brown show through to represent a used wooden floor. Using photographs of the prototype from Green (1997), decals were applied using HMRS Pressfix sheets.

Fig. 65   The wagon on the left has been painted and is awaiting decals to match the completed model shown on the right.

These wagons were originally built by the Cambrian Railways to primarily transport dressed slate from the quarries/mines in North Wales to the rest of the country or to the ports for export around the world. You could consider fabricating a slate wagon load for your finished wagon or, alternatively, resin cast slate loads are available from a number of sources for painting. Scratch building a load could be considered using thin card or plasticard.

CONSTRUCTION OF A BRASS WAGON KIT

Brass kits are generally perceived to be more complicated kits for the more experienced modeller. Typically, these kits require the modeller to provide wheel sets and brass bearings, but generally come with much more detail than would be typically found in a plastic or white metal kit. The level of additional detail and improved running performance of the completed model due to the weight are some of the reasons for making models out of brass. However, it is down to the skill of the modeller, as discussed earlier, and brass kits tend to be more expensive, but when built well and carefully finished off, they do look extremely nice on your layout.

To show the construction of brass kits I have looked at examples that I have made for both part and complete kits. One of the first brass kits that I attempted was the construction of the Shire Scenes GWR W1 Parcels Van. This kit comprises brass body sides, to which you can, if preferred, add brass end walls from the same or another supplier. The kit makes use of the Ratio GWR four-wheel coach kits for a donor underframe and roof, and if not using brass coach ends, you could also re-use the plastic coach ends. The construction of this kit was described in an article that I wrote for *Railway Modeller*, published in 2010, and from this I learned some extremely useful lessons and techniques for working in this medium, which I have highlighted below.

First, the instructions provided with the Shire Scenes kits are straightforward but could do with more detail and illustrations, and whilst they probably make sense to an experienced model maker, they would likely cause some head scratching from a less experienced modeller. It is essential to read all of the instructions before starting any of the work. The brass frets were clean and needed no clean-up of flash, just careful removal, with either a sharp knife

Fig. 66 As a starter kit in brass, the Shire Scenes etched brass body conversion kit to produce a W1 Parcels Van is a good start, making use of a Ratio four-wheel coach for the underframe and roof sections.

Fig. 67 *As part of the construction process, the underframe is shortened and brass replacement end walls added before the brass sides are shaped to match.*

or sharp scissors, of the relevant parts as required. The kit makes up into an excellent model with just the odd dab of cyanoacrylate glue required to hold folded sections in place.

Bending the tumblehome on the lower portion of the coach sides, i.e. the slight inward bend of the bottom of the coach sides, was the only difficult task with the construction of this kit. The instructions supplied with the kit were a bit vague on this process, so I used the following method to accomplish the correct shape to the bodywork. I started by carefully bending the coach sides between my thumb and fingers working slowly from one end to the other. If this is done a small bit at a time and with patience, I found that you can achieve a good, even shape to the body sides to match the correct overall profile required. This was checked against the end profile of the replacement brass end walls to ensure that they would match when brought together to form the body.

Installation of the droplights required careful folding of very small tabs, which when inserted into the preformed holes in the coach sides form the door hinges. To get these tabs folded and the whole assembly shaped to match the inside curvature of the sides, I found to be quite difficult and required a lot of patience to get it right. Once achieved though, the result was worth the effort.

The replacement coach end sections are cut from the fret and the various folds made to the side returns and the buffer beam details, with use of super glue as required, to hold parts in place. Buffers were then added and allowed to harden off before attaching the coach ends to each end of the floor.

The instructions with the Shire Scenes kit state that the floor, sole-bars/side steps and roof from the donor Ratio coach kit will need to be shortened by approximately 8mm. Having measured this before construction started though, I was not convinced this was completely accurate. Therefore, I opted to first fold up the brass section coach sides and ends, and then measure these completed sub-assemblies to get the actual length required for the floor and so on. The amount of shortening may vary depending on the construction of the brass sides and to some degree by the moulded plastic parts of the Ratio chassis kit.

Once I offered up the sides to the floor, I could then determine by how much the floor, associated running gear and steps needed to be reduced. To keep the 'W' irons in the correct position relative to the prototype, I opted to cut a section from the middle of the relevant parts of the underframe, rather than trim a section from each end. I then re-joined the shortened halves together to form the new underframe for the brass kit (see Fig. 67). The method of

Fig. 68 With the body shell completed, the curvature of the sides, referred to as the tumblehome, has been formed to match the end wall profile.

shortening the chassis is not stated on the instructions for the Shire Scenes kit and is an extremely fiddly task that requires patience on the part of the modeller to ensure clean and square joints, as well as to limit damage to the Ratio kit parts.

To achieve the shortened chassis, the floor was measured up with cut lines marked at 49.5mm from each end. A razor saw was used to cut the floor along these lines and then each half filed smooth and square. The two ends were re-joined on a flat glass surface and glued together with liquid polystyrene cement. The floor was then put to one side to dry whilst a similar operation was carried out on the sole-bar/'W' irons and then the side steps. On re-assembly, I found that the axle tie bars and the side steps were quite fragile and I opted to reinforce the joints with short sections of plastic card strip located on the inside of the assembly and thus not visible unless the model is turned upside down and, once painted black, almost invisible. Alternatively, the plastic tie rods could be removed and replaced with suitably sized brass rod.

The axle boxes were drilled out to 2mm diameter to accept the brass bearings, which were fitted before gluing the sides on to the floor. Once fitted, the wheels were installed to check free-running before they were hardened off. Clasp-style brake shoes and other underframe detailing were then added at this

stage and then the entire chassis assembly was then put to one side to harden off.

The same principle of cutting out a central section to reduce the length was also applied to the roof, so as to maintain the end profiles. Cutting the central section out with two cut lines perpendicular to the long axis of the roof ensured that the roof rain-strip detail was not unduly affected. To ensure the correct length for the roof, this operation was left until after the coach ends and sides had been attached to the floor and allowed to set. Before any cutting took place, the moulded gas lamp tops were carefully removed and the roof section filed flat to remove these protuberances.

The roof section was then marked and a central piece about 9mm in length was removed with two cuts of a razor saw. The two ends were then filed on the cut lines and re-joined using liquid polystyrene cement to ensure a 'melting' of the plastic sections into one another and thus reduce the visibility of the joint line on the re-assembled roof. The removed central section was shaped with a craft knife and re-used as a strengthening section on the inside of the roof, under the join line of the two ends. Once the glue had hardened off, the roof joint was carefully filed to smooth out the join line.

Once the underframe assembly had hardened off, the first stage was to attach the coach ends. This was

Fig. 69   A completed GWR W1 Parcels Van conversion with painting, decals and fine details added.

accomplished with super glue and I used small right-angle triangle sections, formed from plastic card on the inside of the model, to ensure that the coach ends were at 90 degrees to the floor and square. Once set, work could then begin on adding the detail parts to end of the coach.

The coach sides were then added and, if the instructions on folding the top side returns are followed, they effectively 'hang' off the side returns from the coach ends. When putting the parts together in a trial assembly, I found that the Ratio plastic floor unit was about 1mm too narrow; so thin, plastic card packing strips were fashioned and glued to each side of the floor to get the correct width. Once satisfied with the fit of the sides, these were then attached with super glue. I found that running the tip of the super glue tube along the join between the bottom of the coach side and the floor also helped to strengthen this joint after the initial fix, as seen in Fig. 68.

Turning to the roof, the shortened section was offered up to the body and fine adjustments made by filing to achieve the correct fit. The positions of the shell ventilators and gas lamp tops were marked

on the roof using the prototype information. Holes were drilled in the roof to accept the white metal replacement components, which were fitted to the roof before painting and final fixing to the body. Before fitting the roof, the body and underframe were painted appropriate colours and glazing added to the door windows (*see* Fig. 69).

Following on from the Parcels Van, I have since completed a number of other kits in brass, including the Shire Scenes GWR Siphon C milk wagon and the 51L GWR Horse Box. The Shire Scenes Siphon C is another body kit similar to the W1 Parcels Van, except that the body is formed from two layers of brass fret and the wagon ends are integral to the kit, not separate additions.

The kit again makes use of the Ratio four-wheel coach chassis and roof, duly modified to the correct length, similar to the process described above for the W1 Parcels Van. The kit costs around £18 and is an extremely good starter kit for those modellers graduating to brass from plastic. Whilst the modifications to the roof and chassis are fiddly, providing care is taken the resulting product is a very good model (*see* Fig. 70).

Fig. 70   *A range of kit conversions is available from Shire Scenes, including the four-wheel GWR Siphon C Van.*

When making up my kit of the Siphon C, I chose to use metal fine-scale wheels running in brass bearings in lieu of the wheels provided with the Ratio coach kit, as well as adding a white metal vacuum cylinder, vacuum pipes and buffers to give the correct pattern to match the prototype and to provide additional ballast weight to improve the running characteristics of the finished model.

In terms of the 51L brass kit of the GWR N6 Horse Box, this kit comes in one large fret, including compensation units for the wheel sets, as shown in Fig. 71. Additional parts also included with the kit

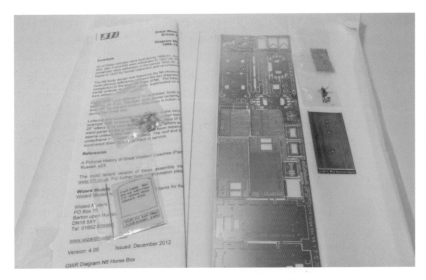

Fig. 71   *An example of a complete brass wagon kit is the etched brass fret for the GWR Horse Box produced by 51L. This kit includes all but a few fine detail parts on a single brass fret. Additional white metal components are also provided, along with a section of plasticard for the internal wall and seating.*

comprise a section of plastic card for the internal walls, turned brass and steel sprung buffers, white metal axle boxes, springs, vacuum cylinder and other detail parts, and a selection of brass wire for the hand rails and brake rods.

A small fret for brass three-link couplings is supplied, although I chose to add small tension lock couplings (Bachmann ref: 36-025) for use on my layout. The couplings and mounting blocks, plus the fine-scale 14mm diameter Mansell pattern wheels and brass bearings were the only components I needed to add to the kit, except paint and decals.

The 51L kit differs from the Shire Scenes kits in that the instructions provided are much more comprehensive and suggest a logical sequence for construction of the kit, as well as some sketches to show some of the key stages in the completion of the smaller detail parts. Rather than describe the construction sequence in detail here, I have just included some additional notes based on my experience, which could be read in conjunction with the instructions supplied with the kit and which may be applicable to other kits.

The first part of the kit to build is the chassis, by folding up the ends and 'V' hangers as already described (see Fig. 72). The buffer shanks are added at this stage and I found it useful to use one of the buffers as a jig to ensure the holes in the shank and bush are aligned prior to fixing. The next stage is the fitting of the internal body sides and the end walls to give a box structure. When adding the end walls, start with the end that has steps, as the lower steps are on the locating tabs of the sidewalls. Once this is square with the sidewalls, then add the other end wall.

Fig. 72   The model is built as a series of layers, beginning with the underframe folded up. The sole bar overlays are added and the buffer beam and buffer shanks fixed in position.

Fig. 73   The inner sidewalls are added to the underframe starting with one long side and then working around the body to form a complete a box structure.

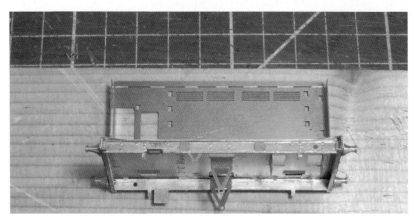

Fig. 74 *The outer sidewalls and the details to the end walls are then added to complete the body. On this model waste brass strips from the fret were used to form additional ballast weight to fix inside the wagon body.*

Fig. 75 *A view of the underside of the completed wagon after application of primer, showing rocking compensation unit to the right-hand side of the image. The underframe detail has been added and the kit is awaiting matt black top coat for completion.*

The key point when fixing the sides together is that the lower tab, bent at 90 degrees, sits on the chassis and slots over the protruding tabs from the sole bar inner. So it is important to make sure that your solder or glue does not flow around the top edges of the tabs protruding through the flow through the floor, otherwise you will have to clean them up to remove excess materials to enable the sides to sit flush on the chassis.

I chose to add ballast to the wagon kit and fixed two brass strips across the middle of the wagon at this stage of the body construction, on which the ballast would be fixed later (see Fig. 74). The next stage of the process was to work on the construction of the underframe detail. When folding up the 'W' irons and clasp brake sub-assemblies for each axle (one rigid and one rocking), be aware of what type of coupling arrangement you wish to fit on to the completed wagon. I use tension lock couplings, so to ensure space for the coupler and mounting block, it was necessary to omit the outer brake block connecting bars and the safety loop.

From my experience, I would recommend that you work slowly and patiently on this type of kit. The parts fix together well, but you need to make sure

that you put them together in the correct sequence. As I have noted previously, use dry runs to test fit and work out the best sequence of construction. During the construction of the underframe details, check fitting and running of the wheels regularly; I found the need to make small adjustments to the brake gear and safety loops.

PAINTING YOUR MODELS

As well as considering the materials and tools required for kit or scratch building, it is also important to consider how you want to paint the completed model, as well as the application of appropriate decals. In this section I will consider some points on painting and provide some comments on decals in the following section.

WHEN TO DO THE PAINTING

The first question is whether to paint before or after construction, and the answer is not always the same. A review of the pros and cons of when to carry out painting has been presented in the table The Pros and Cons of Painting at Various Stages.

THE PROS AND CONS OF PAINTING AT VARIOUS STAGES

Before Construction	
Pros	Cons
• Easier to paint fine detail whilst parts are still on the sprues • Easier to hold sprue and paint detail without getting paint on other parts or details • Enables you to be able to paint internal or hard-to-access parts the right colour	• Where the part is cut from the sprue, it will still need to be touched up with paint • You may need to sand joints and get clean edges on the components so that they will adhere and therefore the parts may need re-painting after the joint has set • Glue marks after construction will need to be touched up
After Construction	
Pros	Cons
• Depending on the quality of mould, cast or etch, and your ability as a modeller, you may have to fettle joints or parts to fit together, and then paint to cover all this over • Cover up glue marks and joint lines with paint	• Some fine detail parts are difficult or impossible to paint when the model has been put together

The comments listed in the table suggest that the best compromise is to paint fine detail and internal components before and external parts after construction. This is where reading and understanding the instructions provided, before you do anything else, is important. If you understand how and when parts are assembled, this will let you identify which parts need painting before building and what can be left until the model is built, or at least largely built.

TYPES OF PAINT

The most common paints used for models are enamels and acrylics. The choice is down to individual choice and preference. Enamel paints are very common for all types of modelling in matt, satin and gloss finishes, and are readily available in a wide range of colours and shades (see Fig. 76). Enamel paints are hard-wearing and for railway modelling many of the railway company paint liveries have been replicated by a number of specialist paint suppliers of enamel paints.

Fig. 76   A wide selection of enamel paints is available for the modeller produced by Humbrol, Phoenix and others. Phoenix produce paints to match numerous railway company liveries. A variety of fine brushes is useful for painting your completed model.

Fig. 77 To bring out fine detail and add weathering effects, it is possible to use a selection of good quality acrylic paints with suitable brushes and mixing palette.

Acrylic paints (see Fig. 77) are also available in a wide spectrum of colours and can easily be blended to produce just about any shade or colour required. Being water-based, I have found that acrylic paints are less hard-wearing, but being relatively quick drying they are excellent for weathering and dry brushing techniques. I tend to use enamel paints for the base colour coats and then sometimes use acrylic paints to highlight details or provide light weathering.

HAND PAINTING OR AIR BRUSHES

I do all my painting by hand with a selection of brushes, with the exception of the use of aerosol paints (generally car body spray paints), which I often use to prime metal components prior to painting. I am pleased with the quality of painting that I achieve by hand painting. It is also possible to achieve excellent finish quality using air brushes. On a personal level, I have always been put off by the cost of an air brush and compressor in the past and have stuck with my tried and tested hand-painting techniques. It is essential for hand painting that one uses good quality brushes and that the brushes are thoroughly cleaned straight after each painting session.

The cost of air brushes and the range available today is considerable and prices have reduced in relative terms as a result of the increasing availability and ranges on offer. However, I have not yet

been tempted to have a go, as I still prefer the hand-painting techniques I have honed building all types of kits over the last thirty years or more. I am sure there will be many readers who will have an equally strong preference for the use of air brushes and the quality of finishes that they can achieve using these tools. At the end of the day, it is down to personal preferences and circumstances.

My advice to a beginner would be to try kit building and use the relatively cheap option of a paint brush first. If you decide to develop kit and scratch building as an area of your railway modelling, then consider investing in an air brush and associated equipment.

APPLICATION OF DECALS

On completion of the painting of your model, the final finishing touch is to add the decals appropriate to the railway company or private owner and period being modelled.

The application of decals is an area where there is likely to be some debate. Many of the kits available today at the less expensive and more straightforward to build end of the market often come with waterslide decals. Generally these decals include the basic company letter, load, tare and a selection of running from which to choose. The more

Fig. 78 To complete the model rolling stock, a selection of Pressfix (produced by HMRS) and/or waterslide decals can be used for company or owner details.

complicated kits for the more experienced modeller tend not to include the decals, leaving it up to the individual to decide on the type and style of decals, based on the time period and area being modelled.

More detailed and expansive sheets of decals are available to the modeller from a number of commercial sources and generally fall in to three main categories: waterslide, Pressfix and Methfix. Out of preference, having used all three types, I prefer to use Pressfix decals and tend to use the sheets available from the Historical Model Railway Society (HMRS), unless it is something highly specialized, for which I may use waterslide decals from suppliers such as Modelmaster Decals or Fox Transfers.

Decal application instructions seem to vary by supplier and, as with kit instructions, it is advisable to read through any instructions before starting work on the kit. For my preferred Pressfix decals, I have a few simple tools that I have to hand when applying decals to my models and would recommend the same:

- Fine scalpel
- Tweezers
- Old paint brush
- Plastic right angle
- Piece of tissue or absorbent cloth
- Finger nail
- Patience

I use a fine scalpel to score around each decal on the front paper and then to carefully separate the front from the backing paper. I always use tweezers to peel off each loosened decal and to place the decal in the desired position on the model. Using a combination of the scalpel and tweezers enables me to fine tune the placement to try and get it exactly correct, with reference to the photographs of the prototype, as discussed elsewhere.

The plastic right angle is used to ensure that the positioning of the decals is square and perpendicular to the base of the wagon, where necessary. It is also useful as a straight edge when positioning numbers or text to ensure that all the individual numbers and letters are aligned.

The old paint brush is used to apply water to the back of the decal once positioned and for fine movement to correct the alignment. Once the backing paper has thoroughly soaked through, the brush is used to remove the backing paper from the decal and to flood the area with water to remove surplus adhesive. The tissue or absorbent cloth is used to mop up the water and press the decal firmly on to the model to ensure that it affixes. I use my finger nail to run gently over the decals where these extend over planking or strapping detail on the wagon body to ensure the decal fits to the contours of the body.

The last element noted above is patience – this is extremely important when fixing lots of decals on your finished model. Do not be tempted to rush, as a crooked line of decals will be obvious on a completed model and it would be a shame to have to scrape off the decals and start again.

CHAPTER FOUR

DETAILING KITS

In the previous chapter I looked at the types of kit available and the methods and techniques for constructing kits as supplied by the manufacturers. In some of the examples described, where I looked at construction sequencing, I also described briefly the use of replacement parts and additional detail components. In this chapter, I will look at the use of replacement components and adding additional detail to your kits to enhance their appearance and perhaps make them that much more unique.

SPARES FROM KITS

When building a kit, you will often find that the manufacturer will provide alternative parts to create different variants of the prototype. These alternative parts should not be thrown away when you have finished building the kit, as they can form the basis of future kit detailing or conversion projects. Being a typical railway modeller, I hoard parts and transfers from old kits in case they come in useful on a future project. I always carefully remove the spare components from the sprues, clean them up and add them to the selection of pieces in my spares' box (see Fig. 79). These spare parts can often provide a useful source of materials for detailing and converting other kits, or they can be used for scratch-building projects.

Although at first glance it might seem improbable that you might find a use for these items in the future, I have found that this source of parts is relatively cheap, having already paid for them when purchasing the original source kit, and they can be readily modified to suit your requirements. (For example, refer to the description of the scratch building of the bogies for the GWR Tourn wagon described in Chapter 7.)

Typical examples of spare parts that I have accumulated over the years include: upright and hanging vacuum pipes; brake gear to suit variable wheelbases; brake levers and vacuum cylinders; coupling hooks, buffers and buffer beams; 'V' hangers; axle boxes and tie bars; van and coach roofs and van end walls.

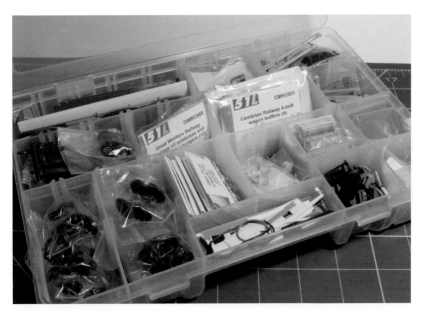

Fig. 79 The spares' box for hoarded parts, specialist components, replacement wheels and bearings and so on, is a fundamental part of the railway modeller's workbench.

In this chapter, I will look at how alternative parts, as well as the hoarded parts saved from previous kits, can be used in the construction of wagon and van kits.

REPLACEMENT BUFFERS AND COUPLING HOOKS

I find that on many kits the supplied buffers and coupling hooks are plastic and sometimes the incorrect pattern for the period that I choose to model. There are numerous specialist suppliers of components for the railway modeller, particularly in 4mm scale, and it is relatively easy to obtain a more appropriate pattern of buffer and cosmetic coupling hooks to replace the ones supplied with your kit.

By selecting white metal or brass components you are also adding additional ballast to your plastic model and helping to improve its running qualities on your layout. Replacement buffers can be bought as ready-made white metal castings or turned brass components; or they are available in kit form as sprung buffers.

I recommend that the installation of these replacement parts is carried out before the ends and sidewalls are fixed together, as it is easier to do this whilst the wagon body can be held flat on the work surface.

I tend to use white metal castings for replacement buffers from a number of different suppliers, such as ABS and 51L, as shown in Figs 80 and 81. To install the cast buffers, take a drill bit held in a pin vice and gently twist with your fingers, or if you prefer use an Archimedes' hand drill, and guide the bit into the holes on the buffer beam. The pre-drilled holes in the buffer beam are used as guidance, so ream out the holes to the correct size for the shank on the replacement part.

For the construction of the Iron Mink van kit that was described in Chapter 3, the buffers and coupling hooks could be replaced with white metal items from the ABS range of components. In this example, the use of the ABS buffers would necessitate creating a 2mm diameter hole through the buffer beam to accommodate the buffer shanks.

When reaming the hole has been completed, the moulded detail on the buffer beam plate can be removed using a fine file at the location of each buffer. The replacement white metal buffers are then removed from the sprues using a side cutter and the shank filed to shape, before gently squeezing the shank into the prepared hole in the buffer beam.

Fig. 80 There are a number of suppliers providing a wide selection of white metal replacement components. Almost any conceivable part required by the modeller is available and it is good practice to have plenty in stock.

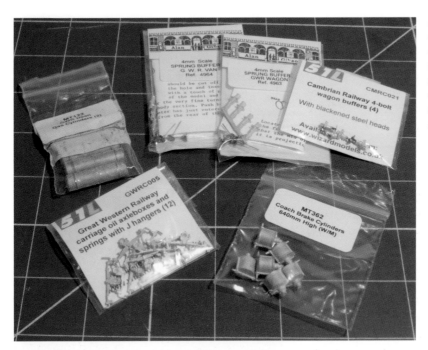

Fig. 81   White metal brake cylinders, axle boxes/ springs and replacement sprung buffers are just some examples of the components that I keep in stock before starting any modelling project.

Fig. 82   To install replacement buffers, use a 2mm diameter drill to ream out the pre-drilled holes in the buffer beam for the replacement buffer shanks.

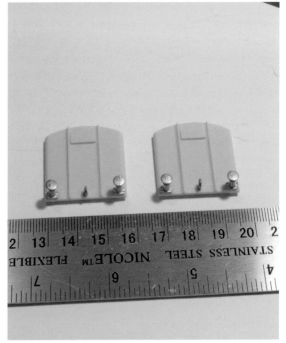

Fig. 83   The replacement white metal buffers and RCH coupling hooks fitted to the van kit have been gently pushed through the reamed out holes and are held in place by the application of impact adhesive at the rear.

With variation in the casting process, the degree of fine filing of the buffer shank can vary and has to be carried out on a trial and error basis to check for fitting in the prepared hole. Do not force the buffer shank through the hole as there is a risk that the buffer beam will be damaged or deformed in the process. Once inserted through the buffer beam, the buffers are held in place with a spot of cyanoacrylate applied on the rear face of the buffer beam and capillary action will draw the liquid into the join between the white metal and plastic parts.

To replace the coupling hooks in the same kit with cosmetic RCH white metal components, the hole for the hook is first checked to see if it will accommodate the alternative white metal component. If not the hole is carefully opened out with a sharp craft knife, the tip of a fine file or a fine drill bit (typically 1.2mm diameter). The hooks are then inserted and fixed in place in the same way as described above for the buffers, as shown in Fig. 83.

The installation of sprung buffers is carried out in a similar manner to the cast buffers, by first reaming out the hole in the buffer beam to the correct diameter to accept the parts. As an example, the installation of sprung buffers on the brass horse box kit identified in the previous chapter was carried out as follows. The cast brass shank was test-fitted in the pre-drilled hole in the buffer beam. Then the bush was fitted to the rear of the shank, on the internal face of the buffer beam. It is important with sprung buffers to make sure that the hole for the steel buffer head tail is correctly aligned through the cast shank and bush, otherwise the buffer will not work.

Using the buffer head tail as a jig, the shank and bush were aligned and fixed together with a spot of cyanoacrylate adhesive. The buffer was removed and the joint between the bush and shank strengthened with further application of the same adhesive. Once fixed, the assembly was tested with the buffer and spring to ensure correct movement before fixing the shank and bush to the buffer beam. On completion of the rest of the underframe, the buffer heads and springs are fed through the cast parts and the tail of the buffer head is bent through 90 degrees to secure in position.

Fig. 84 A wide selection of more prototypical replacement wheels is available in OO gauge from various suppliers. If planning to use replacement wheels, make sure these are ordered and kept in the spares' box in advance.

REPLACEMENT WHEELS

Many kits these days are supplied with metal wheel sets, but not all, especially if you pick up an older kit from an auction site or from a stall at a model railway fair, as these will often be supplied with plastic wheel sets. Whilst the plastic wheels will work satisfactorily, the running of the wagon or van will be greatly improved by the use of metal tyre wheels running in brass bearings, as these provide weight, give better running qualities and adhesion to the track.

Sometimes you may find that where metal wheel sets are provided in a kit, they are not necessarily the correct pattern for the particular company, or period, being modelled and thus ought to be replaced with the correct pattern. Good quality metal tyre wheels are available from a number of suppliers in 4mm scale, such as Alan Gibson or Romford.

Fig. 85 Utilizing a brass back-to-back gauge to check the accuracy of the replacement wheels before installing them in your model. It is also good practice to use the brass gauge to check wheels on RTR stock, as this is often the cause of poor running.

Before starting your kit, if you have decided to purchase replacement metal wheel sets, it is advisable to check the back-to-back measurement on each set prior to fitting, as this is essential for good running quality on your layout. Selecting the track for your layout will influence the choice of wheel sets; for example, OO gauge, EM or P4 are all modelling at 4mm scale but to differing degrees of accuracy. I model at 4mm OO gauge fine-scale and tend to use the wheels produced by Alan Gibson for the rolling stock that I make. I have always found these wheels to be well made and accurate in terms of back-to-back measurements.

As an aside it might be useful to briefly explain the concept of back-to-back measurement. The measurement refers to the distance between the back of the wheel flanges on rolling stock. On RTR stock this can be variable and certainly on older rolling stock the flanges were extremely thick and 'coarse scale' by modern standards. Today the bulk of RTR stock runs on much finer scale flange wheels, looking less

toy-like and more model railway like! This allows the use of stock on finer scale track that looks much more realistic.

I choose to model in OO gauge, but adopt finer scale principles such as the use of fine-scale wheels from the Alan Gibson range, running on PECO Streamline Code 100 track. I could use Code 75 track, but that would mean re-wheeling many older items of RTR rolling stock, which I occasionally like to run on the layout. This would not only cost a significant sum of money but also detract from the value and character of the older models, but this is purely a personal choice.

Therefore, back-to-back measurement for OO gauge should be 14.5mm on a track gauge of 16.5mm; whereas for EM it should be 16.5mm (track gauge of 18.2mm) and for P4, 17.75mm (track gauge of 18.83mm). Further information on the differing approaches in 4mm-scale modelling offered by OO, EM and P4 can be found on the respective society websites.

To install metal wheel sets in your rolling stock kits you first need to decide on the pattern of wheels and supplier. On my rolling stock, as I have stated previously, I tend to use OO gauge fine-scale wheels sets from the Alan Gibson range, but other makes are available. Each set of wheels will require brass bearings fitted in each of the axle boxes. Starting with the bearings, these are fitted by first reaming out the axle boxes using a 2mm diameter drill bit.

This must be done extremely carefully to prevent damage to the axle box and I tend to do this by gently twisting the drill bit backwards and forwards using the bit held securely in a pin vice or between your first finger and thumb. I also recommend that this exercise be carried out whilst the axle box and sole bar are still attached to the moulding sprue, as this provides some protection to the fragile parts during the process.

The depth of reaming can be checked by dropping the brass bearing into the axle box and checking that the shoulder fits flush with the rear face of the axle box. When the fine adjustments have been completed, each bearing cup can be fixed in place with a spot of cyanoacrylate adhesive dropped in

Fig. 86   The use of replacement wheels is best accompanied by the use of brass bearings for the pin-point axles. Installation of the brass bearings is accomplished by reaming out axle boxes with a 2mm diameter drill bit.

Fig. 87   It is important to check the depth of reaming prior to fixing brass bearings in place, to ensure a flush fit of the bearing to the inside face of the axle box.

to the axle box and the bearing pushed home. With the bearings fixed, the construction of the kit can proceed and the wheel sets dropped in to check all is square.

It is advisable to leave the wheel sets in place until the underframe components have hardened off and typically I like to leave mine overnight to ensure the adhesive has securely fixed. The axle boxes can then be gently sprung apart to remove the wheel sets whilst the rest of the kit is completed and painted.

FITTING COMPENSATION UNITS

A further improvement in the running qualities of your rolling stock can be achieved by the installation of compensation units at one or both ends of the wagon. The unit rocks independent of the wagon body and underframe, thus providing a suspension element to ride over uneven track and maintain wheel contact with the rails.

Typically the compensation unit is an etched brass fret that is folded up into shape and then fixed to the bottom of the wagon. For some types of units the structure typically comprises two parts: a base plate, which is securely fixed to the underside of the wagon, and a pivot or rocking plate, which sits onto lugs bent up from the fixed base plate. Once connected, the lugs are bent over to lock the pivot plate in position, while allowing it to rock from side to side, as required. If desired, these units can also be built up as rigid units, typically by folding up a stop bar on the base plate to prevent rocking.

Other types of pivot units utilize folding tabs on the floor of the wagon and on the unit, which have been pre-drilled with a hole through which a short piece of wire (typically 0.7 to 0.9mm diameter) can be threaded and used as the pivot bar for the plate.

The brass bearing cups are fitted to the compensation units in pre-drilled holes and the wheels sit in their bearings located within the compensation unit and are independent of the axle boxes on the wagon, as shown in the photograph in Fig. 89. The compensation unit shown in the photograph was used for the white metal kit described in Chapter 3 and can be made as either a rigid or a rocking unit.

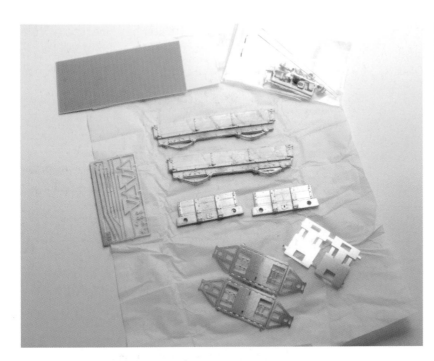

Fig. 88   A typical metal wagon kit comprising brass and white metal components, with the etched brass rocking unit at the bottom of the figure.

Fig. 89   The etched brass compensation units are folded up and secured to the separate base plates using the fold-up lugs passing through slots in the unit. The lugs are then twisted to stop the unit becoming free.

Fig. 90   An alternative type of rocking compensation unit on the GWR Horse Box kit produced by 51L utilizes a 0.9mm diameter wire threaded through the unit and locating fold-down flaps on the wagon floor.

Fig. 91 *The plastic van kit as produced by Colin Ashby to be used as the starting point of the wagon detailing described in this section.*

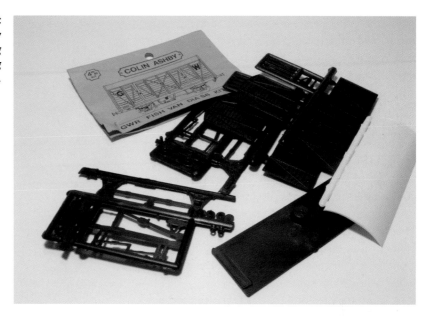

DETAILING A VAN KIT

To show how a van kit can be detailed I have used a worked example of a kit for a GWR Fish van to Diagram S6, produced by Colin Ashby, which I believe may no longer be in production, but the principles adopted here apply to other van kits. A kit of the same wagon was also available as an Ian Kirk kit in the past (before the range was sold to Colin Ashby, I believe) and both examples of the kit can occasionally still be picked up on eBay for a modest price.

The kit as supplied includes all the parts required to construct the body and underframe; the modeller is expected to provide wheels, bearings, couplings, paint and decals. I built one of the Ian Kirk kits some thirty years or more ago and this still runs on my layout today, alongside the more recent example constructed from the Colin Ashby kit. The earlier example was built as per the kit with just the addition of upright vacuum pipes as extra detail. The later model has been more heavily detailed, as described in the worked example below.

PREPARING THE PARTS

Construction of the kit began with carefully removing the main body sections and roof from the sprues, for which I used a fine-tooth razor saw. The use of the razor saw in preference to a craft knife allowed more control of the removal process and did not

Fig. 92 *The preparation of bodywork should be undertaken in the same way as you would when building any wagon or van kit of this type.*

stress the joints between the parts and the sprue that would otherwise have occurred with a craft knife and risk damaging the parts. The parts were then cleaned up to remove flash from the moulding process and the sprue connecting points, so that they were ready for building.

The buffer beams on this van kit are part of the end wall sections and include moulded buffer shanks. Plastic spacer rings and buffer heads are provided in the kit to make up the buffer assembly. I was not convinced that these represented the pattern of buffer that I wanted to use on the finished model. Therefore, I chose to remove the moulded plastic buffer shanks carefully with a sharp craft knife and then, using a fine needle file, removed the moulded buffer plate on the buffer beam.

A 2mm diameter drill bit was then used to bore through the buffer beam at each location to accommodate the replacement white metal buffers that I selected for this kit. A third hole was drilled in the central buffer beam plate with a 1.2mm diameter drill to accept the white metal cosmetic coupling hooks.

Fig. 94 Using a 2mm diameter drill bit, the next step was reaming out the pre-drilled holes in the buffer beam for the replacement buffers and then using a fine file to remove any moulded detail.

Fig. 95 Fitting replacement white metal buffers should be undertaken carefully. Test fit the white metal shank in the reamed hole and, if necessary, file the shank down. Do not force the part through the hole as this will stress and distort the plastic buffer beam.

Fig. 93 The decision to use replacement white metal buffers required the removal of the moulded buffer shanks with a chisel blade craft knife.

Fig. 96   Re-profiling the moulded axle box tie bar utilizing needle files helps to obtain a thinner profile and appears more realistic.

The underframe required some work with a sharp craft knife and needle files to remove flash and to reduce the thickness of the axle tie bar to a more realistic scale size. Alternatively, this piece could be removed and replaced with a piece of 0.5mm diameter brass wire, if preferred.

The axle boxes were reamed out to 2mm diameter to accept the brass bearing cups and then the underframe parts were removed from the sprue, again making use of the fine razor saw, as described for the removal of the body sections.

BODYWORK AND UNDERFRAME CONSTRUCTION

Following the instructions supplied, I proceeded by first fixing one sidewall and one end together, ensuring that the joint was at 90 degrees. This required some preparatory work with fine files before fixing. A dry run of this type of joint is recommended before fixing with liquid polystyrene cement, to check that the mitred corners meet squarely and without gaps.

The next step was to fix the floor to the sidewall and end wall, ensuring that the lower face of the floor was flush with the bottom edge of the sidewall and at the same time sat level with the top edge of the buffer beam. This required some gentle tweaking to get it right, but once satisfied that all was square, I left the body to harden off on a glass tile, supported with wooden blocks to prevent the body moving or twisting.

When the first section had set, I added the second sidewall and end wall as before. I found that the floor section was slightly shorter than the gap between the end walls. This demonstrates where dry runs and fine adjustments to the wall joints may be necessary, to check that the joints are all square and level. If you are still left with a small gap, as in this case, the gap can be packed using a piece of microstrip fixed on the end of the floor section. When the body had been fixed together, it was set aside and left to harden off.

Taking the sole bars, it was important to check the length of these parts against the space on the body between the back of the buffer beams. It was necessary to adjust the length of the sole bars on this example, which must be done at the same end for both sides to ensure that the axle boxes remain in line. To achieve this accurately, the easiest method I have found is to place the two sole bars back to back and offer up to the body kit. Mark the required reduction in length and cut both sole bars at the same time, keeping them clamped together. If the reduction in length is more than a millimetre or two, it is advisable to cut a small bit from each end of the sole bars to ensure that the axle boxes remain proportionally the same distance from each end of the wagon.

When cut to the correct length, I took one of the sole bars and fixed it to the underside of the body along the alignment of the joint between floor and sidewall. The exact position of the sole bars depends on the length of axles used in the wheel sets and is governed by the back-to-back measurement. A dry run is useful to make sure that the overhang each side of the sole bars is the same, i.e. the underframe is located centrally under the body and not to one side. A useful check is also to put the wheel sets in position to ensure that axle boxes are square and that

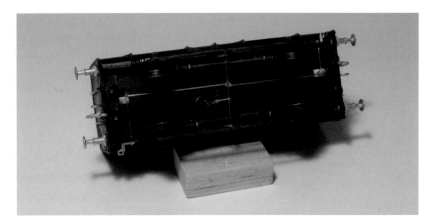

Fig. 97 Detailing of the underframe using fine wire and etched brass wagon detailing components, such as the ones supplied by Mainly Trains for the 'V' hangers and cranks.

Fig. 98 White metal components for vacuum pipes and DC brake levers provide additional underframe detail.

the wheel axles are perpendicular to the sidewall of the body. The second sole bar should be added and the wheel sets put in place to check correct alignment and free-running. The whole assembly should then be left to harden off.

FITTING BRAKE GEAR

The next stage was to clean up the brake gear parts from the kit and test fit on the underframe to check the alignment of brake shoes and wheel treads. On the side of the wagon where the moulded vacuum cylinder is on the floor, I found that the brake gear was pushed too far out of alignment with the wheels for this to be acceptable to my eye.

Using a sharp chisel blade on my craft knife, a thin slice of the vacuum cylinder was removed on the

outer edge, facing the brake gear assembly. Further fine adjustment was made with files and the brake gear test-fitted again to check alignment. Repeat this process, if necessary, removing a thin sliver of the cylinder at a time until the brake gear lines up with the wheel treads. When satisfied with the alignment, fix in place with liquid polystyrene cement.

ROOF ADJUSTMENTS AND DETAILING

Whilst the brake gear was setting, I check-fitted the roof to the body. I found that this part did not fit squarely with the end walls of the van, where an obvious gap was present. To reduce the gap between the top of the end walls and the underside of the roof, I needed to carry out quite a bit of adjustment,

Fig. 99 To ensure a good fit of the roof to the body, a dry run of the assembly identified the need to file down the tops of the sidewalls and to add microstrip to correct the end wall profile to match the roof.

Fig. 100 The prototype van had shell vents fitted on the roof for ventilation. To replicate this on the model, white metal shell vents can be used to detail the roof, using line-drawings to locate the correct positions.

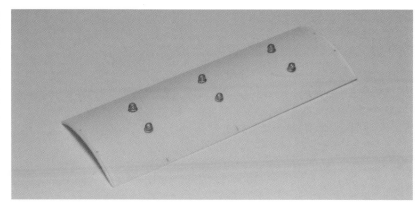

utilizing fine files, to the sidewalls and the roof. The height of the sidewalls was reduced uniformly and then the ridge on the underside of the roof where this sits on the sidewalls was also filed to reduce the height. When this was completed, I found that there was still a small gap of approximately 1mm between the top of the sidewall and the underside of the roof. This was solved by fixing microstrip to the top of the end walls and gently filing this down, checking the fit with the roof frequently to ensure that too much is not removed.

When happy with the fit of the roof, I then set about checking the roof profile and adding detail, specifically the shell ventilators in the roof. The wagon roof on the prototype had two rows of shell ventilators along the alignment of the end wall vertical bracing, equally spaced about the long axis centre-line of the roof. Using the line-drawing of the wagon reproduced in Atkins *et al.* (2013) as

reference, I marked out with a pencil the centre-line of the roof then the corresponding points for the tops of the vertical bracing on each end wall, as the ventilators are positioned along the same alignment. I then placed the long edge of the roof against the line-drawing and marked on the edge of the roof the points where the ventilators were fitted. Using a rule and pencil it was then possible to mark out the six locations of the ventilators, where the construction lines crossed.

With the locations of the ventilators marked, I drilled a 1mm diameter pilot hole at each location, re-checked the locations and then reamed out the holes to 2mm diameter to accept the shank on the underside of the white metal ventilator components. For this model, I used ABS white metal components, as the white metal adds a bit more weight to the overall wagon to address the issue of weight and plastic models (discussed in Chapter 2).

Fig. 101 An element of wagon and van kits not often modelled is the retaining loops to the brake gear. A close-up of the etched brass brake gear retaining loops added to this model.

The six ventilators were pushed home through the holes in the roof and aligned correctly using a photograph of the completed prototype wagon as reference. A spot of impact adhesive (UHU) was used on the underside of the roof at each shank to hold the parts in place. The roof was set aside to dry whilst further detailing was undertaken to the wagon body.

UNDERFRAME DETAILING

The next bit of detailing to the body was the addition of cast white metal Dean Churchward (DC) brake handles in lieu of the ones supplied in the kit. These were carefully cut from the cast sprues, cleaned up with a fine file and fixed in place with a spot of cyanoacrylate adhesive.

Replacement white metal vacuum pipes were added to the end walls, fixed with a spot of glue to the end wall and the underside of the buffer beam to ensure a secure hold. Etched brass label clips from a Mainly Trains wagon detailing kit (MT 166) were then fixed to the left-hand end of the sidewalls of the van, about four planks up from the sole bar, checking against a photograph of the prototype (Atkins et al. 2013) to get the correct position.

With the brake gear hardened off, the next stage was to add a representation of the brake linkage using etched brass 'V' hangers and cranks (Mainly Trains kit MT 230) and 0.5mm-diameter brass wire.

Fig. 102 This end view of the wagon shows that all of the modifications to the end wall have been completed, using various materials and components.

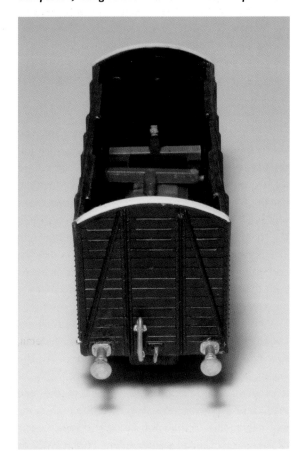

Fig. 103   Completion of the underframe detailing showing the use of etched brass and white metal components.

Using a 0.5mm diameter drill, I carefully drilled a hole in the centre of the plastic brake gear crank, supporting the plastic part on a piece of wood to prevent it breaking whilst drilling. A piece of the brass wire was then threaded through the hangers and crank to form the connecting rod. This allowed the alignment to be checked of the 'V' hangers on the rear of the sole bar on each side of the wagon, as well as the crank for the vacuum cylinder.

Once satisfied with the alignment, a small spot of cyanoacrylate will hold the 'V' hangers and crank in place; further adhesive can be dropped on to the joints to strengthen them, as described in Chapter 3. When these parts have been secured in place, the connecting rod was fixed with a spot of cyanoacrylate on the 'V' hanger and then the wire was trimmed to length with side cutters.

Before adding the remainder of the brake linkage, I opted to install on the underframe the small mounting blocks, which I use for the types of tension lock couplers that I use on my rolling stock. Once these had been set in place, I then set about using parts from my spares' box and more 0.5mm diameter wire to create a representation of the brake linkage between the hand brake handles and the central connecting rod. To do this, it is important to have the wheel sets in place, to check that the linkage rods do not inhibit movement of the wheels and axles, as this will affect the running qualities of the finished wagon.

With the hangers, rods and connecting bars to the vacuum cylinder formed from plastic rod in place, this completed the underside detailing, except for the addition of brake gear retaining loops. These were formed from etched brass parts suitably bent in to a 'U' shape and fixed just behind the brake shoes, as seen in Fig. 103.

FITTING ACCESS STEPS

The final part of detailing on this van was the addition of the side steps below each of the doors. On the prototype, two steps were provided at each location to allow access to the van from both platform level and from ground level, such as when being loaded or unloaded at a quay. The model was supplied with steps to reproduce this feature of the prototype. The first stage was to fix the upper steps in place on one side of the van, as these affix directly to the sole bar and can be quickly aligned and set below each door.

With the top step firmly fixed in place, I then offered up the lower step and checked its position directly below the upper step. The lower step fixes to the axle box and was held square by two connecting rods with the upper step, although the parts for the connecting rods were not supplied in the kit — the modeller is required to supply plastic rod or wire to form these parts. The lower steps provided with the kit have to be modified with a cut-out to allow

Fig. 104 Once all of the modifications and detailing has been completed, the roof is test-fitted to ensure all is finished prior to painting the model.

it to slot around the axle box. This is best done by checking the step alignment with the upper step and then marking on the inside edge of the lower step with a pencil the position of the axle box.

Using a sharp craft knife, two small cuts were made from the back edge of the step perpendicular to the edge for a depth of approximately 1mm. I connected the two cut lines with a third cut, then tidied up and made adjustments with fine files to get a snug fit around the axle box and so that the two steps were aligned vertically one above the other. This was a bit of a trial and error process to get the right fit, so I only removed a small amount of material at a time and kept checking the fit and alignment. I found that it is best to complete the steps on one side of the wagon first and let them harden off before turning the wagon over to start the second side.

I would recommend that fitting the connecting bars is best done after the steps have been fixed in place and the glue hardened off. On the model that I built thirty years ago, I used plastic rod for the connecting bars between the steps, whereas on the more recent model I used brass wire, which I believe gives a better scale-size effect on the finished model.

Inside the wagon I wanted to add more weight to improve the running quality of the model, so I used some curtain hem weights obtained from the local haberdashery shop. The weights supplied were slightly too long for the van, but could easily be cut with a sharp heavy duty knife, such as a Stanley knife. The weights were supplied in small plastic bags, so sealing the weights in the bags I then fixed the bag with impact adhesive to the floor of the wagon. To prevent the risk of these coming loose over time, I used some sections of plastic sprue cut to the correct length as braces across the top of the weights and fixed to the internal sides of the sidewall with liquid polystyrene cement.

FINISHING TOUCHES

At this stage, the wagon was now ready for painting. I always leave the roof separate from the body whilst painting for ease of holding. The underframe was painted matt black and the body was painted coach brown to represent a wagon during the 1920s and 1930s to match the period on my layout.

The roof was painted coach white and left to dry fully before fixing to the body. When fixing the roof in place, liquid polystyrene cement was applied to the top of the body walls and then the roof held in place with elastic bands for at least twelve hours to allow the glue to fully harden off.

Fig. 105 A common problem with plastic wagon kits is that over time there is a possibility of the sidewalls bowing inwards. An effective method of preventing this happening is to install internal bracing using scrap pieces of sprue. Also visible in the figure are the additional ballast weights wrapped in plastic and fixed to the inside floor of the van.

Fig. 106 The use of photographs of the prototype is essential to ensure the correct locations and detail of decal placement after painting of the wagon and roof in appropriate colours. An additional internal brace for the top of the sidewalls is also shown in this figure.

Fig. 107 The completed and detailed van with correct livery and decals in accordance with the official prototype photographs of a GWR Fish Van to Diagram S6.

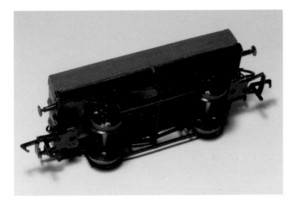

Fig. 108 The application of underframe details equally applies to open wagons as to vans. In this example of a British Railway 10T open wagon, the use of etched brass parts, wire and plastic rod to complete the detailing can be seen.

DETAILING OPEN WAGON KITS

As with the detailing of van kits described earlier in this chapter, the detail to the underframe of an open wagon is very similar in principle, comprising the inclusion of brake gear and linkages, as well as brake levers and, where applicable, vacuum brake equipment, but this is dependent on the prototype being modelled.

Detailing of the body of an open wagon can include the addition of etched brass corner plates and rivet strip details to improve the moulded representation of the kit, as well as the addition of door hinges, load-securing rings and other fitments. Fitting of the etched brass components is described further in Chapter 7 as part of the scratch-building of the Tourn open wagon. Further detailing of open wagons lies with the addition of loads, a representation of how these loads were secured and, where necessary, covered for transit. These detailing options are considered further in the following sections.

ADDING LOADS TO OPEN WAGONS

Open wagons rolling up and down the railway network would not always be empty in the real world, as empty wagon movements cost money in that they do not provide a return against the cost of movement. In this way, if you wish to represent real railway practice on your layouts, wagons running on your layout should also not be running up and down empty all the time. In this section I have provided some ideas as to how you can easily and relatively cheaply provide wagon loads for open wagons to represent this practice on your layout.

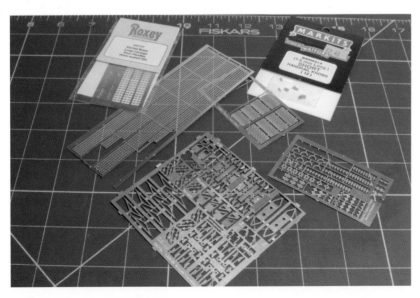

Fig. 109 Some of the more common brass detailing items available include etched brass rivet strip, corner plates and brake gear for wagons, as well as door handles for vans and coach stock.

Adding a Coal Load

During the early part of railway history in the United Kingdom, one of the principal purposes of railways was to carry raw materials, such as coal and minerals, to support the industrial development of the country. Up until the early part of the twentieth century, these materials were typically carried in wooden-bodied open wagons and formed a significant part of the rolling stock inventory of both the railway companies and the private collieries and mines. Although I have described this as adding a coal load to an open wagon, the same principles apply to other minerals, just utilizing different coloured materials.

To insert a coal load into a wagon, first decide whether you wish to make this a permanent addition or a removable load. In the example described here, I decided to make the load a permanent addition in a Cooper Craft loco coal wagon. To form the load I first inserted a raised floor into the wagon, which

allows you to add additional ballast weight under the raised floor should you so desire.

The floor was formed from a piece of thick artist card, measuring approximately 62mm by 27.0mm, cut to be an exact fit to the inside of the wagon body. These dimensions will vary from wagon to wagon and for each wagon that you wish to add a load, it will be necessary to measure the internal dimensions once constructed.

To bring the false floor up to the desired level in the wagon, packing pieces can be cut from the same thick card and stuck directly on to the wagon floor, if the load is intended to be permanent. For a load that you wish to remove, then a base piece can be cut to the same size as the false floor on which the packing pieces can be fixed. The 'new' floor is then stuck in place on top of the packing pieces.

I tend to use white PVA glue to fix card to plasticard and then stream a thin line of white PVA around the edge of the floor and the walls to seal the join

Fig. 110 Providing wagon loads in open wagons is part of making your layout look more realistic. If you do not want to fill the wagon completely, adding a load can be made easier by the installation of a false floor formed from card and fixed in to wagon, as shown.

Fig. 111 Before adding the load, in this case coal, the false floor was painted a dark charcoal colour to match the colour of the proposed load so that no white card was visible through the added load when complete.

Fig. 112   When the false floor has been completed, the wagon load can be added. The load is held in place on the false floor with PVA glue, which is best applied with a brush.

Fig. 113   It is a good idea to ensure that the PVA adhesive is worked into the gap between false floor and sidewall of wagon to help secure the floor to the wagon side to prevent bowing.

Fig. 114   Using a small spoon apply the material forming the load to the wet PVA glue. Build up the thickness of the load by applying further PVA and material. In this instance the 'coal' is formed from shredded cork dyed black, but real crushed coal could be used as an alternative.

Fig. 115 A completed wagon with decals and load looks very effective and provides a touch of realism to your model railway layout.

if it is a permanent load. Once dry, the new raised floor is then painted black or dark charcoal grey and allowed to dry.

Select the material you wish to use, which could be real coal crushed to size, but in my case I used shredded cork painted matt black. The load was glued in place using a watered down white PVA-type glue, which when dried provided a glossy sheen on some of the faces of the cork particles, representative of what you would see with real coal or anthracite.

A similar approach can be used for other aggregate or crushed rock loads, adjusting the colour of the false floor to match or closely resemble the colour of the material that is being transported.

Adding a Timber Load

During the steam period of our railway heritage, in particular, the transport of wood and timber on the railways was a significant operation. A browse through old photograph collections and books will reveal images such as imported hardwoods being transported from ports to mill, sawn timber transported from mills to local goods yards and the transport of timber props for the coal-mining industry.

To make timber loads for open wagons I have found the best source of material to represent sawn timber is the various drink stirrer sticks you can pick up free with your take-out coffee, or lollipop sticks

available from any homeware store. These ready-made pieces of sawn timber can be cut to any width or length to suit the wagons that you have running on your layout. The wood can then be either left natural, or can be painted, or treated with varnish to represent different types of wood.

A further example of a wood load for wagons is to provide a representation of pit props or telegraph poles. To form these types of materials, I have found that the wooden barbeque skewers from the supermarket can be readily adapted and then varnished or painted accordingly.

The accompanying photographs show some examples of timber loads in both standard and long wheelbase wagons and you will note that in the standard 10ft wheelbase open wagon the timber has been loaded following prototype practice so that it rests on the end wall at one end of the wagon. This type of detail all helps to create a realistic model railway, mimicking practices from the real world. This is easily achievable and the result of researching through photographs of freight operations on the railways can provide you with valuable information on the way various materials were loaded and transported.

SECURING WAGON LOADS

On the 12in to the foot railways, wagon loads were held in place in open wagons using chains, ropes or wagon tarpaulins, or a combination of these

Fig. 116 Timber loads were a typical wagon load of the steam era and this open five-plank wagon is shown prototypically loaded with timber planks formed from recycled coffee stirrers.

Fig. 117 For longer wheelbase open wagons, the opportunities for larger loads can be considered. The wagon on the left is loaded with planks, whilst the one on the right has a load of creosoted posts, formed from barbeque skewers cut to length and suitably painted with acrylics.

methods. The same ought to be represented on the models that you recreate in 4mm to the foot scale.

Ropes

To represent ropes, I tend to use brown or dark-coloured threads 'borrowed' from my wife's sewing box. The thread can be twisted together to make thicker ropes if required and can be bent and stuck in position with PVA type glue. It is important when fixing the threads in place on your model that they are laid out in the same way that a real wagon is loaded and the load secured.

Reference to prototype photographs will provide a valuable source of information to show how

tarpaulins are wrapped at the corners of wagons (or not) and the way that loose, uncovered loads are secured with ropes.

Chains

For heavier loads, chains would have been used instead of ropes and you can buy fine chain from a number of suppliers to represent load-securing chain in 4mm scale, such as the examples shown in the photographs to retain timber (see Fig. 117) and steel girder loads, on the respective wagons.

However, you can also make use of old necklace chains, which can be picked up very cheaply at second-hand shops. Once washed and tarnished, or

Fig. 118   Loads need to be securely fastened to wagons and in the case of the timber plank load, the load has been retained using rope formed from twisted threads.

Fig. 119   For heavier and more substantial loads, chains are required. In model form these have been modelled using fine thirteen links to the inch chain available from a number of modelling suppliers.

even spray painted if preferred, these can provide very realistic loading chains.

Tarpaulins

Tarpaulins can be either made or bought ready formed for use in 4mm scale. I have used the tarpaulin sheets produced by Roger Smith, which are a good way of representing a loaded wagon without having to make a load to fit the wagon. It also allows you to put additional ballast weights in the wagon under the tarpaulin, if desired.

If you cannot get the correct tarpaulin sheets for your models or you want a cheaper alternative to buying ready-made ones, then you can always make your own. This can be done in a number of ways

using tissue-type paper, coloured and lettered to the correct detail for your period.

The method I prefer for making tarpaulins is described below using tissue paper collected from all sorts of packaging, particularly the sort you get when buying china or glass, as well as the new tissue you can buy from any stationers for wrapping presents.

First take a sheet of tissue paper large enough to make at least one wagon sheet plus an extra centimetre or so around the edge. Select the colour of the sheet that you want – I chose a dark charcoal grey (Humbrol Enamel Matt 67) and using a reasonably large modeller's brush (No. 5) apply a coat of paint to one side of the sheet of tissue paper, with strokes working on one direction across the sheet.

Fig. 120   The use of tarpaulins was once widespread on open wagons. The GWR Open A wagon fitted with a sheet rail has been covered with a weathered wagon tarpaulin produced by Roger Smith. The securing ropes have been formed from twisted threads.

Fig. 121   The LNWR open wagon is loaded and covered with a homemade tarpaulin sheet formed from painted tissue paper. Here again, the tarpaulin is secured with ropes made from twisted thread.

Do not be too fussy about brush strokes, or if the paint does not quite cover the entire sheet.

Set the sheet aside to dry thoroughly for at least twenty-four hours. Turn the sheet over and then paint the other side in the same manner, but with the brush strokes at 90 degrees to the direction of brush strokes on the first side. Again do not be

too fussy about streaks or brush strokes as this all adds to the effect of a weathered and heavily used tarpaulin sheet.

Leave the second side to dry for at least twenty-four hours before thinking about any further coats of paint, although I have found that a single application of paint per side was sufficient. When the paint has dried, add any numbering or letterings as desired using decals or drawn by hand. In the example shown here, I opted to leave the sheet blank.

Whether you make your own or buy ready-made tarpaulin sheets, each tarpaulin looks more realistic if it is then gently scrunched up then folded out again to represent a used sheet, prior to fixing over the wagon body using thread as rope ties, forming ropes as described earlier.

The tarpaulin can be applied directly to the wagon sides or you may wish to add a 'load' under the sheet that sits proud of the top of the wagon sidewalls. To form the load under the sheeting in the example shown, I used pieces of thick card folded and fixed to the bottom of the wagon with glue. Once the load has set, take the tarpaulin sheet and fix with PVA type glue to the top surface of the card load and leave to dry before progressing further. Check before fixing that the tarpaulin sheet will extend to the wagon sides when folded down around the load and adjust as necessary.

When the sheet is securely fixed to the load, work your way around the wagon, folding the tarpaulin sheet around the load and then, using the same glue, fix to the wagon body, starting with the long sides first, before fixing to the end walls. It is useful at this stage to have a photograph of a wagon loaded and covered with a tarpaulin to show how these covers were placed over the loads, folded at the corners and tied in place. I then used short pieces of khaki cotton thread to represent ropes between the sheet and the wagon body, copying the pattern of tying from pictures of the prototype.

READY-MADE WAGON LOADS

A number of suppliers, such as Ten Commandments, Dart Castings and others, provide a range of ready-made wagon loads in resin, plaster or white metal that can be painted as required. These ready-made parts are a good way to save time in making things for your model railway and for making a wagon load that maybe is a bit more complicated to fabricate. The quality of the products is generally very good, with little need to clean up flash before priming and painting.

The only down side to this approach is that these items tend to come at a cost, which if you are working to a tight budget may be prohibitive. In this instance, using your imagination and a bit of wood or modelling clay you can create a wide variety of objects to represent wagon loads, as well as be creative.

WAGON DETAILING COMPONENTS

Although the quality of wagon kits supplied today is generally excellent, on some of the older kits the detail of the moulding is limited. For those that like the minutiae in fine detail, or when scratch building, it is possible to obtain detail kits, generally brass frets, covering all sorts of fine detail items to adorn and enhance your kit, RTR model, or scratch build project.

Some examples of the types of components that can be obtained include riveted wagon strapping, corner plates and maker's plates, as seen in Fig. 109. The use of these components is best done by reference to prototype photographs to show location and layout. The use and fixing of these types of components has been described earlier in this chapter and in more detail in Chapters 6 and 7.

WEATHERING

The subject of weathering can be, and has been, the subject of complete books by others more competent than I in this area of modelling and I would refer you to some of these other texts for detailed accounts of weathering techniques, paints, powders and other weird and wonderful techniques for turning your pristine models into replicas of the real world rolling stock.

Suffice to say that I do not personally weather my models particularly heavily, if at all, as I prefer the out-shopped look to my rolling stock, with perhaps just a very light weathering on the underframe. To achieve the look I want, I use dry brush techniques utilizing various enamel and good quality acrylic paints to get the subtle tones. To get the right effect it is advisable to work from a photograph of the prototype to observe the distribution of the weathering effects across the wagon. In the application of dry brush techniques, I use very little paint and work a little bit at a time to see how the effect develops on the wagon.

USEFUL SOURCES OF MATERIAL

When looking for parts to detail your kits, RTR or when scratch building, there are many useful sources of materials for detailing without spending a fortune. This is starting to verge on scratch building, which is discussed more in Chapter 6, but I have included some discussion here as it refers specifically to detailing of wagons.

By way of an example, one excellent source of fine brass-coloured wire is the wire mesh that can be found around wine bottles, in particular, certain brands of Rioja and Chianti wines. This is a good excuse to buy a bottle or two, consume the contents with dinner, then after dinner spend an hour or two carefully unwinding the wire into a single coil for re-use. This material is great for making fine pipework; for example, as used on the Cordon Gas Tank wagon or for door bolts on the Siphon F wagon, both of which are described in more detail in Chapter 7.

Another extremely useful source of material for detailing is staples, available in various sizes and can be used as a cheap material for a number of uses. For example, I have used staples bent and re-shaped to represent handrails and grab handles on wagons, coaches and scratch built narrow-gauge locos.

APPLICATIONS TO YOUR RTR FLEET

The detailing methodologies discussed in this chapter have been primarily aimed at working with wagon kits. However, there is absolutely no reason why these detailing techniques could not also be applied to detailing RTR models to make your rolling stock fleet that bit more unique.

If you are a bit uncertain as to whether you want to start work on your pristine and carefully assembled RTR rolling stock collection, why not buy a cheap, old, second-hand wagon from a show sale stand, or on-line, and use this as a test bed for ideas and practising your techniques. If it works, then great – you have breathed new life into an old model; but if it does not work, then at least you will not have damaged that expensive new rolling stock!

CHAPTER FIVE

KIT CONVERSIONS

INTRODUCTION

The purpose of this chapter is to provide the reader with some inspiration and ideas as to how to go about creating wagons for their layout through conversion of commercially available kits. When putting together the notes for this chapter, it occurred to me that the most appropriate way to demonstrate how to go about converting kits was to provide a selection of worked examples of kit conversions to show what can be achieved in a series of relatively simple steps.

I have undertaken a number of conversion projects and I have selected a series of five examples, which are described in this chapter. Some of these examples are based on a number of short articles that were published in *Railway Modeller*. I have taken these articles, and revised and expanded the text to demonstrate ideas for techniques that could be used on a wide variety of projects.

The principles discussed in the examples provided in this chapter, with respect to conversion of kits, can be widely applied to other prototypes and scales. In addition, it is also possible to consider conversion of RTR models and so, at the end of the chapter, I have also included a worked example of how this process can be applied to converting RTR rolling stock.

CONVERSION 1: CREATION OF A SMALL CATTLE WAGON

BACKGROUND

The inspiration to build an example of this type of small cattle wagon came from a photograph I spotted in Beck (1986: 93) whilst reading about the history of the railway lines around Oswestry and Gobowen, specifically the lines of the Cambrian Railway and Great Western Railway. The photograph of this

Fig. 122 *Two completed examples of the short cattle wagon conversions of Cooper Craft kits, showing the application of decals and weathering on the finished models.*

unusual prototype was intriguing and represented something a bit different to the standard cattle wagon available from the RTR manufacturers and existing kit suppliers. I will describe how I built a model version to 4mm scale and will provide some useful hints and tips should anyone wish to try a similar exercise.

My first step was to carry out further research on this particular prototype and I began by referring to a copy of Russell (1971) to see if this book had any further information about this prototype. Researching through this text, and some of the other books in my collection, I found several different photographs of a similar prototype, as well as a line-drawing of a similar version of a small cattle wagon.

Kit and RTR versions of the larger W1/W5 cattle wagons (GWR telegraph code Mex) are readily available from various sources. What is not readily available at the time of writing is a version of the small cattle wagon described above, presumably because there were not as many prototype examples.

I had considered scratch building from raw materials, but an alternative to a complete scratch build was to undertake a conversion of a readily available cattle wagon kit. To achieve this conversion, I made use of the Cooper Craft kit (ref: 1010W) as a starting point, a kit that is particularly attractive for the detail on the parts and which is suitable to be used for the planned conversion.

There was no scale drawing for this specific version of the small cattle wagon in Russell's book, however, there is a drawing (1971: 28) showing an earlier type of cattle wagon, albeit with external framing, but of a wagon of similar size to the subject prototype, indicating a 9ft wheelbase. Studying both the photographs and the available drawings for some time allowed me to determine how the conversion could be achieved. I settled on using a 9ft wheelbase and altered the sides of the Cooper Craft kit accordingly, to create a wagon with an overall length of approximately 14ft (equating to about 56mm in 4mm scale).

As part of my deliberations as to how to carry out the conversion, I made notes of possible materials to use and where and how to make the cuts to the kit to obtain the relevant sections required to complete the modified wagon. The following kits

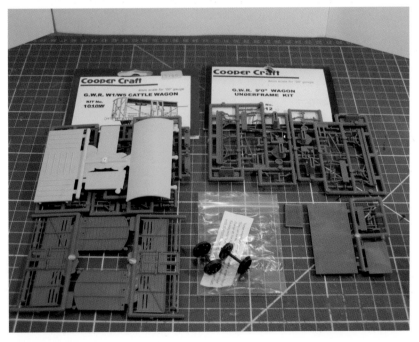

Fig. 123 *The conversion requires two separate Cooper Craft kits to make one wagon. A standard cattle wagon kit and the 9ft underframe kit provide the main parts.*

and components were assembled before any of the work could proceed:

- Cooper Craft kit 1010W GWR W1/W5 cattle wagon with metal wheels and brass bearings included (these can be sourced elsewhere if an earlier version of the kit with plastic wheels is used)
- Cooper Craft kit 1012 9ft wheelbase under-frame kit
- Various pieces of plastic card/strip as required for strapping
- Waste white metal for additional ballast

CONSTRUCTION OF THE UNDERFRAME

To begin with, all of the parts from the two kits were laid out on my work bench and studied to identify which items would be required for this con-version project and what could be recycled to the spares' box for use on other future projects. The sides, ends and roof sections were required from the cattle wagon kit, whilst the wagon floor, sole bars/axle boxes, brake gear, buffers and hooks came from the underframe kit. For the purposes of this project I decided to retain the plastic buffers and coupling hooks supplied with the kits, instead of replacing them with white metal prototype reproductions, as I felt that the items supplied were good enough, but that can be left to personal preference.

Comparison of the dimensions of the sole bar sup-plied in the underframe kit to the photographs of the prototype indicated that the length of the sole bar on the prototype was only slightly longer than the point at which the suspension springs join the sole bar at the outer end of each side. No scale drawings were available to confirm actual dimensions in the litera-ture that I had researched, so I decided to cut the sole bar at each end and reduce the overall length to about 54mm (approximately 13ft 6in in 4mm scale).

This appeared to compare favourably with the photographs of the prototype in terms of propor-tions and relative distances between the leaf springs/axle boxes and the back of the buffer beams. Once happy with the dimensions of the modified sole bars,

Fig. 124 *The first stage was to shorten the floor and sole bars to match the length of the prototype wagon.*

both sides were placed back to back to ensure that the axle boxes lined up and any fine adjustments were made with fine files. The sole bars were then offered up to the wagon floor section, which was marked accordingly and cut to match the length of the modified sole bars, using a razor saw.

MODIFICATIONS TO THE SIDEWALLS

The next task was to modify the sides of the cattle wagon to match the length of the shortened wagon floor. Before any cutting took place, a careful exami-nation of the parts as supplied with the kit showed that the wall panels either side of the central door were divided into two sections, separated by verti-cal strapping and with a diagonal strap running from the bottom of the door to the top of the sidewall at the wagon end. The small Mex prototype shown in the photographs that I used for this project only had diagonal strapping from the bottom of the door

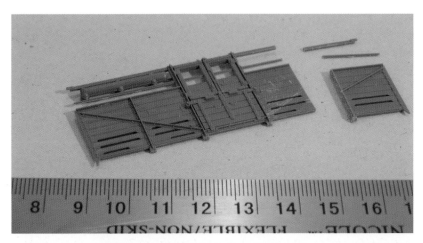

Fig. 125 The sidewalls were cut and angle iron detail was removed using a chisel blade craft knife.

Fig. 126 The shortened and then reassembled sidewall at the bottom of the picture compared to the partially shortened sidewall at the top demonstrates the surgery required to the kit.

to the top of the wall at the wagon end and did not have any vertical strapping in this area.

The access door to the wagon needed to be central to the body side, so the wagon sides needed to be shortened by the same corresponding amounts either side of the door to match the modified floor. At the same time it was important to remember to allow approximately 1mm overhang each end to tie into the mitred joint with the wagon end walls. To carry out the shortening exercise I opted to make vertical cuts in the walls on the door side of the vertical strapping, as shown on the enclosed photographs (*see* Fig. 125). The diagonal strapping was then carefully removed with a sharp chisel blade knife/scalpel and the surface filed flush, after which the planking was re-scribed as necessary with a sharp craft knife.

From the removed section I then measured approximately 6mm from the outside end in order to retain the end detail strapping and mitred joint. A second vertical cut was then made in the sidewall at this location. When carrying out this type of procedure, it is important that the precise length of section needs to be checked against the wagon floor,

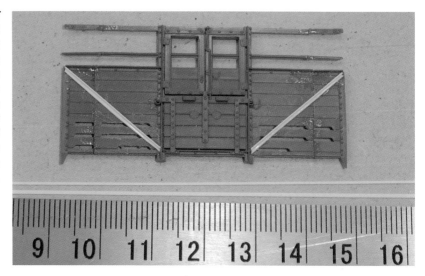

Fig. 127   The use of plasticard microstrip is useful in many ways when kit and scratch building. Here it has been used to form the new diagonal bracing to the wagon body. One piece was laid flat on the wagon body and a second piece was fixed at 90 degrees to create the impression of angle iron detail on the wagon.

Fig. 128   With the modified sides re-assembled, the wagon body and underframe can be constructed as for a standard kit, with brass bearings added to the axle boxes for the replacement wheels.

as there is bound to be variation depending on the accuracy of cutting. I found the use of a fine tooth razor saw essential for this work.

As shown in the photograph in Fig. 126, the two modified sections were then glued together and left to harden off. The retaining bars at the top of each side were then cut and shortened accordingly to match the walls. This whole process was subsequently repeated for each section of wall either side of the central doors.

Once the modified sides had hardened off, new diagonal strapping was fashioned from plastic microstrip to form an 'L' section to match the existing strapping profile. This strapping was added to the walls, as shown on the photographs of the model, during construction. Etched brass wagon strapping could be used if preferred for this process, instead of the plastic strip.

Once happy with the modifications, construction of the parts could then proceed in the normal way for a kit of this type. Brass bearings were installed in the axle boxes before the sole bars were attached to the floor. The wagon ends and sides were then fixed together and checked to ensure that the structure was square, before attaching to the floor. Scrap pieces of plasticard were used on the internal surface of the walls to strengthen the modification joints. To ensure good running, additional weight (scrap white metal) was glued to the floor inside the wagon before the roof was fixed in place.

CHANGES TO THE KIT ROOF

The roof supplied with the cattle wagon kit also needs to be shortened to match the length of the modified wagon, unless a new roof is made from raw materials, such as brass sheet or thin plasticard. The actual length of roof required is likely to vary slightly depending on how accurately you have cut and reassembled the parts. So I would, therefore, strongly recommend that the roof is modified after the modified wagon body has been fixed together. To do this, the roof should be offered up to the completed body shell, marked as appropriate, taking care to retain the roof detail at each end, and then cut accordingly.

Fig. 130   Using the moulded ridges on the roof as a guide, the roof was carefully cut using a fine razor saw.

On the example that I built, this was accomplished by making two cuts in the roof to remove the central panel and one of the central ridges, as shown in Figs 130 and 131, reducing the overall length of the roof

Fig. 129   The original roof has to be shortened to match the new body. To do this the roof was laid alongside the converted body and a pencil used to mark the cut lines.

Fig. 131   The roof was cut into three sections and the central section of roof discarded. The cut joints on the two end sections of roof were cleaned up and bonded together with liquid polystyrene cement.

Fig. 132   The new, shortened roof was test-fitted to the wagon to check for correct length and fit to the end walls. Fine adjustments can be made using needle files at this stage.

by approximately 16mm. The two roof sections were then sanded and re-joined to form the new roof, with the ridge conveniently disguising the new joint in the roof.

FINISHING TOUCHES

Before affixing the roof to the body, the whole body and underframe was painted in GWR freight wagon grey. The internal sides of the walls and floor were painted off-white and weathered to represent use

Fig. 133   The completed wagon was then painted internally and externally. Note the application of white weathering to the inside and around the sidewall vents to represent the prototype practice of using lime wash to disinfect wagons after use.

Fig. 134 *The application of appropriate decals was completed with reference to photographs of the prototype and then the painted roof was fixed to complete the model.*

of lime and general wear and tear. The roof was painted white and then fixed to the body shell. The model was completed with HMRS Pressfix transfers, as shown in Figs 133 and 134.

CONVERSION 2: SHORT PYTHON FROM A PARKSIDE DUNDAS KIT

BACKGROUND

This second conversion project was stumbled upon whilst looking through my collection of books for a prototype photograph of a Siphon F for reference during construction of an old Keyser kit. I came across a couple of photographs in my copy of Russell (1990) of an intriguing vehicle, referred to as a 'very short "Python" to DIA. "P.7"'. One photograph was of a vehicle used as a CCT (Covered Carriage Truck) and the other

was noted from the caption to be in use as a 'Loco Accumulator van'.

I already had an example of the Python A, constructed from a Parkside Dundas kit some years ago. A quick check of the existing model I had with the photograph indicated that there was a possibility of using the standard Python kit as the basis for a conversion to create this shorter version. Another Parkside kit was thus duly purchased and the following notes and accompanying photographs provide some guidance as to how to carry out this kit conversion exercise.

LIST OF MATERIALS REQUIRED

The following kit and component items were sourced and collected together before attempting this conversion project:

- Parkside Dundas GWR Python covered carriage wagon kit (ref: PC 37)

Fig. 135   An unusual prototype spotted in a copy of Russell (1990) led to the construction of this example of a very short covered carriage truck (CCT).

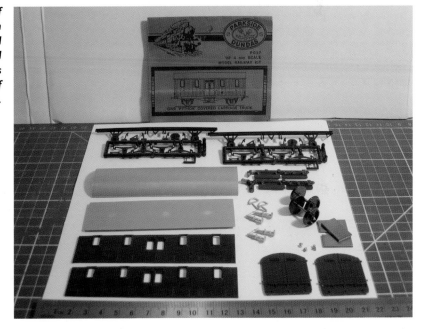

Fig. 136   The contents of the Parkside CCT kit with additional white metal replacement buffers and hanging vacuum pipes formed the starting point of this conversion idea.

- GWR long fitted wagon buffers (ABS white metal or similar)
- GWR hanging-type vacuum pipes (ABS white metal or similar)
- Various pieces of plasticard and plastic microstrip
- Coopercraft wagon weights for additional ballast
- Phoenix paints GWR freight wagon brown and coach roof white
- HMRS Pressfix transfers

The Parkside kit came complete with metal wheels and brass bearings, so there was no need to source new ones, unless one wishes to replace the plain 14mm disc wheels with the Mansell-type disc wheels.

I used replacement white metal long fitted wagon buffers in lieu of the brass buffers supplied with the kit, because in the photograph of the prototype it was coupled to an open wagon and the buffers appeared to be identical to the standard wagon buffer for fitted vehicles, not standard coach buffers.

Comparison of the kit parts to the photographs suggested that the wheelbase for this vehicle was about 9ft, possibly slightly less. This is based on the following two assumptions: first, the vertical planking used on the prototype was the same width as that represented on the model; and, second, that this vehicle was fitted with the standard coach wheels as the Python A, which in 4mm scale are represented by the 14mm disc wheels/Mansell disc wheels. Comparing these elements with the photograph seemed to suggest the correct proportions.

The vertical planking on the prototype, as shown in the photographs, comprised ten vertical planks either side of the central double doors. When checked against the dimensions of the axle springs supplied with the kit, this compared favourably with the position of the wheels and springs in the photograph. The prototype had no windows in each sidewall or in the side doors, and furthermore had no vents in either the end doors or over the doors in the sidewalls.

MODIFICATIONS REQUIRED TO THE BODY

Once happy with the assessment of the suitability of the kit parts for this conversion, I then set about deciding how to shorten the sidewalls and remove the windows. I decided to start at the central doors,

Fig. 137 The original kit required shortening. The sidewall was careful measured and marked prior to cutting with a fine razor saw.

Fig. 138 Each sidewall was cut into nine pieces, from which five pieces, including the central door section, are required. The windows in the doors are in-filled to match the prototype.

Fig. 139   The five pieces are reconstructed to form the new and shortened sidewall required for the kit conversion.

Fig. 140   A comparison of original sidewall, marked prior to cutting, with the reconstructed shortened sidewall, showed the significant difference in length of the two wagons.

which I assumed to be the same width as the Python A version, from which I counted out three planks each side of the door and marked the next vertical joint as cut lines. Next, to retain the end bracing detail of the sidewalls of the model, I counted in four vertical planks from each end and again marked the next vertical joint as cut lines. This provided seven planks either side of the door, so to ensure the correct number of vertical planks I then marked

out a three-plank section between the pair of side windows each side of the door.

Before cutting the walls, the vents above the central doors were carefully removed with a sharp chisel blade craft knife and use of fine files, so that the area was flush with the surrounding walls. The next job was to blank off the windows in each of the doors. For this a small piece of 20thou plasticard was cut, approximately 11.0mm by 5.5mm, to fill each hole. Each blanking piece had the corners rounded off with a file and checked for fit before fixing with liquid solvent. Once fixed in place, the surface of each blanking piece was flooded with solvent to flow into any gaps between the window side frames and the filler piece.

The cuts in the sidewall were all achieved by first using a sharp craft knife and steel rule to score the cut lines. Then, a fine-tooth razor saw was used to make the cuts. As you can see from the accompanying photograph (Fig. 138), you should be left with five sections of wall, including the central doors, to make up the length of the modified body. The rest of the pieces of sidewall were not required for this model and were placed in the spares' box for future use.

Each of the joint edges was carefully filed and checked with a right angle to ensure that they were square before joining using a liquid solvent. To ensure the re-formed sidewalls are flat and true, the use of a flat glass tile on which to place your work is essential during this process. To strengthen the joints in the sidewall, a piece of 20thou plasticard, approximately 5mm by 50mm, was cut and glued along the back of the wall sections at the level of the top of the doors. The bottom edge of the sidewall was strengthened when attached to the wagon floor.

As can be seen from the accompanying photographs, because of the number of cut lines and thus joints that are necessary to form the sidewalls, a combination of cutting and cleaning of the joints will probably result in minor variations in the wall length. To overcome this I found it necessary to use some microstrip added to the outer ends of the walls to ensure that both sidewalls were the same overall length. The amount of microstrip required will depend on the degree of accuracy achieved during cutting of the joints. Place the walls back to back to check dimensions and add the microstrip as required.

The modification to each end wall of the model was less arduous to complete. The vents at the top of each door were removed in the same way as described above and the planking of the doors re-scribed over the modified area with a sharp knife. The buffer mounting plates were filed flat, the holes in the buffer beam were widened out with a 2mm drill bit, and the replacement buffers fitted and held in place with a dab of impact adhesive on the inside face of the wall. The coupling hooks supplied with the kit were also added at this stage.

The hinge detail of the end doors on the prototype was different to that represented on the Parkside kit of the Python A vehicle. On the two photographs that I have of these vehicles, the end doors were full length, each with three hinges on each door. Plates over each buffer, similar to that seen on the Serpent-type open carriage wagon, were present on one prototype vehicle but not the other. The detail on the kit was representative of the more standard Python vehicles, in that the end doors were

Fig. 141 After re-constructing the sidewall the joints were filled, where necessary, using liquid polystyrene cement. The vents above the doors were removed using a chisel blade knife and sanded smooth with fine grade sandpaper.

Fig. 142   The end walls of the CCT required the removal of the vents at the top of the doors and the installation of correct pattern replacement buffers.

shorter, had only two hinges per door and there was a lower drop-down section that fell over the buffers.

After examining the kit parts, and in particular the depth of moulding detail for the lower drop-down section, I was not confident that this could easily be modified other than by completely removing this section and replacing with new plasticard, suitably scribed with plank and hinge detail. Given that there were already a number of joints in each sidewall, I wanted to keep the end walls in one piece to provide some strength and rigidity to the body of the model. On this basis I decided that it was an acceptable compromise, in terms of accuracy, to leave the end door arrangement as per the original kit and provide rigidity to the body of the wagon.

MODIFICATIONS REQUIRED TO THE FLOOR SECTION

The floor section from the kit needed to be shortened to match the modified body. I would recommend that the modifications to the floor are carried out once the alterations to the sidewalls have been completed. Before making any cuts in the floor section, I found it helpful to check how the original kit goes together before making any changes, and to keep this in mind during the construction of the modified parts. For example, it is important to realize that the floor should be shorter than the length of the

sidewalls, as the ends of the wagon kit sit inside the sidewalls.

With this in mind, I offered up the modified side-walls to the floor and marked accordingly. Looking at the bracing detail on the underside of the floor, I decided to start from the mid-point of the long axis of the floor and mark out the length of the modified

Fig. 143   The van floor was measured against the new sidewalls and marked accordingly. The floor was cut to length with a razor saw.

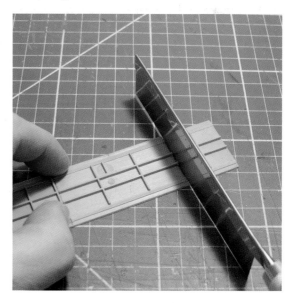

section. On my example the cut lines for the shortened floor fell just within the second cross-bracing counting out from the centre of the floor section, giving a modified floor length of approximately 57mm.

The floor was then cut using a razor saw and the new ends of the floor cleaned up with a file. Some minor trimming of the longitudinal bracing on the underside of the floor at each end might be required to enable the floor to butt up squarely against the end wall sections. As with all kits of this type, a dry run with the joints was a useful way to see if any fine adjustment was required before fixing.

MODIFICATIONS REQUIRED TO THE SOLE BARS AND UNDERFRAME

The sole bars of the modified wagon were approximately half the length of the original kit and the same length as the modified floor section, at about 57mm. Examination of the photographs of the prototype showed that there were no DC brake handles on each side of the wagon, as per the 'standard' Python vehicle, as the axle springs extended to the ends of the sole bars and butted up against the back of the buffer beam. I followed the instructions from the kit for the installation of the brass bearings and then the fixing of the axle boxes and springs to the sole bars.

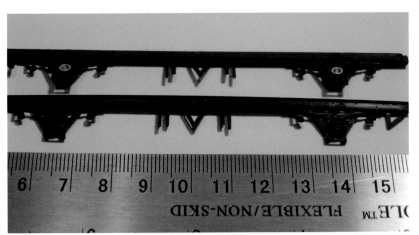

Fig. 144 The original sole bars from the Parkside kit with brass bearings fixed in axle boxes.

Fig. 145 To get the correct alignment of axle boxes for the new van, the sole bar was cut into five pieces.

Once the springs were stuck to the sole bar and had hardened off, I cut each sole bar into a number of pieces, as shown Fig. 145. This comprised the sections where each axle box/spring assembly was located; a central section from each side that had the fixing points for the steps, 'V' hangars and underframe detail; and finally two short end-pieces, from the original end of the sole bar to the point where the outer end of the axle springs met the sole bar. The two short end-pieces and the central section are not required for this modification, with the exception that the detail from the central section of the original sole bar was carefully removed with a sharp knife for re-use on the modified kit. The two pieces over the axle boxes and springs were measured and cut to be approximately half the length of the new floor (approximately 28.5mm).

The photographs of the prototype that I have do not clearly show the detail of the underframe. Therefore, I assumed that the 'V' hangars and vacuum cylinder were used on these vehicles as per the layout on the original Python kit. In terms of the brake connecting rods, the photographs of the prototypes showed that the brake connecting rods were external to the underframe. The rods passed across the front of the axle boxes, with short connecting rods to each brake shoe. These could be replicated with fine wire on the model, but I was concerned that this might be impractical and prone to damage during handling for use on my layout and, therefore, I opted to omit these fine details from the model.

MODIFICATIONS TO THE ROOF SECTION

As with the floor, I would recommend that the modifications to the roof are carried out once the body of the vehicle have been completed. I wanted to retain the end profile on the roof as supplied with the original kit, as this sits over the end walls and there was a lip on the underside of the roof that butts up against the inside face at the top of the end wall.

The internal dimension between the inside faces of the end walls should be the same as the modified floor section, but to check, this was measured and

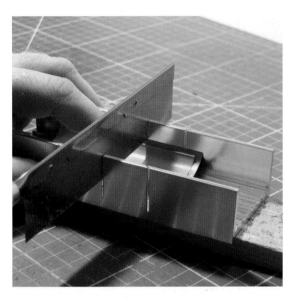

Fig. 146   With the body completed, the roof was marked and then cut with a razor saw. For this cutting job, the roof was held securely in a bespoke cutting block for the razor saw.

found to be approximately 57mm. I then measured half the length of the distance between the end walls (approximately 28.5mm) from the lip on the underside of the roof at each end. This gave two cut lines and the roof was cut with a razor saw.

The two end sections were then joined using a liquid solvent to 'melt' the plastic either side of the joint. When hardened off, the roof joint was lightly sanded to smooth out the line of the joint flush with the rest of the roof.

CONSTRUCTION OF THE MODIFIED PARTS

Once all of the modifications had been completed, the parts of the kits were then put together using the instructions from the original kit for guidance. The walls and floor were fixed together first to form the body, before adding the sole bars and underframe detail. When it came to adding the sole bars, I started at one end of the floor and fixed two sections of sole bar with the axle boxes attached to both sides of the floor at the same time, making sure that the bearings were aligned squarely with each

Fig. 147 With the body under construction, bracing was applied to the internal face at the top edge of the sidewalls to support the wagon body.

Fig. 148 The modified body and underframe construction completed, showing the required use of microstrip at the ends of the sidewalls as described in the text.

Fig. 149 There was little prototype information available on the detailing of the underframe. On the model the underframe detail is largely guesswork based on studying the detail on numerous other wagons and vans.

Fig. 150 After the roof has been cut to remove a central section, the two ends were bonded together and test-fitted to the van.

other. The wheel set was inserted at this point to check that the wheels ran freely and that the axle was perpendicular to the sides of the wagon. I then repeated this process, fixing the other two parts of the sole bars, as shown, and inserting the second wheel set.

Hanging-type vacuum pipes were fixed to the buffer beam with a spot of super glue, making sure that the hanging pipe would not interfere with the coupling. Adding the individual brake shoes for each wheel required minor modifications of the pieces as supplied with the kit, to ensure that they could be accommodated around the floor bracing and be in line with the tyres of the wheels. The vacuum cylinder and connecting rods should be added after the brake shoes, as I found that the cylinder required some minor modification to sit over the part where the brake shoe assembly was fixed to the floor.

The final piece to complete the underframe was the addition of couplings. I use tension lock couplings on my rolling stock, but found that the 'Hornby'-type mounting block supplied with the original kit could not be accommodated on the underside of the model as there was insufficient room between the wheels/brake gear and the back of the buffer beam. I, therefore, used cut-down small Bachmann couplings mounted on a modified block that sits between the wheels, as shown in the accompanying photograph.

When completed, the wagon body was painted GWR freight wagon brown, with matt black underframe details, whilst the roof was painted GWR coach roof white, as shown in Fig. 152. HMRS Pressfix transfers were then used to complete the model. The tare figures are my best guess from the information I had, as the quality of the photographs was not great and the numbers hard to read, even with a magnifying glass!

Although I had to make a number of compromises in terms of fine detail, when compared to the photographs of the prototype that I have, I was pleased with the overall impression of the converted model.

Fig. 151   The provision of access steps adds to the creation of a representative model. Steps from the original kit were adapted and fitted to the underframe.

Fig. 152   Application of the appropriate paint scheme, with GWR freight vehicle brown (Phoenix Paints) above a matt black (Humbrol) underframe.

Fig. 153   Pressfix (HRMS) decals added using photographs for guidance. The roof was painted white and fixed in place.

CONVERSION 3: ADAPTING A PECO WONDERFUL WAGON KIT

BACKGROUND

The PECO Wonderful Wagon Kits have been around for many years and I am sure many readers will have had a go, at one time or another, putting one together. The kits are relatively simple to make and provide a free-running and nicely weighted wagon, which if you wish to build straight from the box would probably take no more than about an hour to put together and run on your layout.

I described the construction of the Royal Daylight version of the PECO tank wagon kit in Chapter 3. Here I describe how I took one of the milk tank

wagon kits and, through a relatively simple conversion process, created a tank wagon more prototypical for my home layout.

The inspiration for this conversion project came from the desire to recreate a Great Western Railway tank wagon to run on my branch-line layout, using a readily available kit as the source material. Researching the prototype, in particular with reference to my copy of Russell (1971: figs 169 and 172), this indicated that the kit could provide a reasonable basis for recreating the GWR prototype.

The conversion process described makes use of the kit instructions as provided and I have indicated where deviation from the standard instructions is required should you wish to reproduce the modified wagon shown in the accompanying photographs.

Fig. 154 *Milk tank wagons provide an atmospheric addition to a branch line layout. In model form this has been recreated by the adaptation of a PECO Wonderful Wagon kit.*

LIST OF MATERIALS REQUIRED

To undertake this modification you will need the following kit and component parts:

- PECO Wonderful Wagon Kit (PECO ref: R-74U) United Dairies Tank Wagon
- 20thou plasticard and a selection of plasticard microstrip
- White metal hanging-type vacuum pipes (optional)
- HMRS GWR wagon insignia (Pressfix)
- Matt black paint (Humbrol 33 or similar) for the underframe and modified sections

CONSTRUCTION OF THE CHASSIS

Commence construction of the wagon kit as per the supplied instructions and make up the buffer beam and coupling sub-assembly with your choice of couplings; I used the tension lock couplings as that is what I use on my model railway. The parts go together well straight from the box with little or no fettling required, just a dry run, then fixing with the appropriate adhesive.

When assembling the sprung buffers, I found that when put together, a tiny drop of super glue between the end of each buffer shank and the buffer spring helped ensure that the two parts did not separate, without hindering the performance of the sprung buffers. The next stage was to attach the metal 'W' irons to the main chassis component and then the sole bars, as directed in the instructions.

Fig. 155 *On the prototype, the bottom of the tank was boxed in, unlike the donor kit used here. To achieve this in model form, longitudinal slots were cut into the underframe to accommodate plasticard strips.*

DEVIATION 1 FROM STANDARD KIT INSTRUCTIONS

The first modification of the kit was to take a fine fret saw and on the main chassis section, locate the central tank supporting ribs and cut 1mm-wide slots, as shown in Fig. 155. The purpose of cutting the slots was to allow the addition of a piece of 20thou plasticard strip, approximately 4mm high by 66mm long, to represent the boxing in around the bottom of the tank, as per the prototype and as shown in Fig. 156.

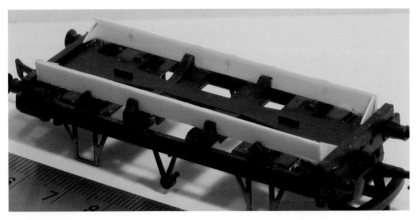

Fig. 156 *Plasticard was cut to fit to form the boxing-in around base of tank body and fixed in the slots. The wedge pieces at each end were shaped to match the curvature of the tank body.*

Fig. 157 Tie bars were added to the axle boxes using microstrip to match the profile of the metal 'W' irons provided with the kit.

The slots should extend through the ribs, so that they are flush with the cross-member of the chassis, such that when the box section is added it sits flush along the chassis, as shown in the accompanying photographs. Small wedge-shaped pieces of the 20thou plasticard were then cut to fit at each end of the tank, as shown in Fig. 156. I found that the cutting and shaping of these pieces was a bit of trial and error to get a neat and flush fit to the base of the tank.

The box section and underframe and chassis, as well as the end supports for the tank, were then painted matt black, to provide a uniform base colour for the wagon chassis. When dry the tank body was fixed in position, as described in the instructions, and the end frames added. The filler cap on the tank was painted black as per the prototype.

DEVIATION 2 FROM STANDARD KIT INSTRUCTIONS

The second main change to the standard instructions was to add a tie bar between the 'W' irons to match the prototype arrangement. I used a piece of plastic microstrip to the same dimensions as the 'W' iron metal frame (see Fig. 157), fixed with a spot of cyanoacrylate (super glue) at each end and then painted matt black to match the rest of the chassis.

DEVIATION 3 FROM STANDARD KIT INSTRUCTIONS

The third modification to the kit was with regard to the installation of the tension rods along the long axis of the tank body. The kit has both horizontal and diagonal tension rods provided, whereas the prototype that I was attempting to construct only had diagonal rods. The horizontal wires were thus omitted from the model.

The finer grade wire for the diagonal bracing was then inserted through the pre-drilled holes in the end frames and fixed at the sole bar as per the instructions. Leaving approximately 1mm of wire protruding through the end frames, the wire was then cut and a drop of super glue used to hold in place, as shown in Fig. 158.

COMPLETION AND FINISHING TOUCHES

The wagon was then completed as per the standard instructions, adding the ladders, strap buckles and inserting the wheels. In addition, I chose to add hanging-type vacuum pipes (ABS white metal or similar) as per the prototype, as well as adding a fine horizontal tie rod between the end frames, as shown in Fig. 159. I opted to use the plastic wheels supplied with the kit, but should you prefer you could replace these wheels with fine-scale metal wheels, such as the eight-spoke wagon wheels supplied by Gibson or Romford.

Once the construction and painting were completed, I then added appropriate decals using the photographs in Russell (1971) for guidance, as shown in Fig. 158. On reflection, this is a relatively quick and simple adaptation of a free-running kit that gives a pretty fair representation of the prototype.

Fig. 158 *A side view of the tank wagon showing the layout of the diagonal tension rods and the underframe painted matt black to hide the plasticard modifications.*

Fig. 159 *An additional end tie bar was added to the tank framing using brass wire to match the prototype.*

CONVERSION 4: CREATION OF A GWR SHORT 13 TON BRAKE VAN (TOAD)

BACKGROUND

The next two conversions described in this chapter show variations on the construction of brake vans, specifically GWR vehicles for my layout, making use of the Ratio GWR 20T brake van kit as the source material. These sections are based on short articles that I have previously published (Tisdale 2012c and 2013), but expanded here to provide more details and photographs to show the processes followed in each example.

Looking at photographs of GWR layouts in the modelling press, at exhibitions or as generally depicted in texts on the subject, the 'standard' GWR brake van, referred to in the telegraphic code as a 'Toad', is typically represented by a van with a veranda at one end, albeit of varying dimensions. This is the image that one normally associates with

Fig. 160 A short 13T brake van based on a Ratio Models kit of the standard 20T brake van.

the tail end of a GWR freight train. However, variations to the standard Toad did exist, but these do not seem to be often modelled or, if they are, not often seen.

RTR models available at the time of writing follow the standard Toad structure, usually the 16T or 20T varieties. Examples of the short wheelbase, the six-wheel heavy (24T), or the odd non-standard Toads, either built away from Swindon or absorbed into the GWR fleet as a result of Grouping, are not readily available as RTR models in 4mm scale.

A number of different kits are available for some of the variations of the standard four-wheel Toad. The six-wheel version is also available as a brass kit (supplied by Falcon Brass), but to my knowledge there are very few, if any, for the non-standard vehicles, with the exception of a couple of examples produced as brass kits, also in the Falcon Brass range.

From a commercial point of view, I suppose the argument would be that these models would have limited appeal and thus are not viable to produce in large numbers. Therefore, this means that to model one of these non-standard vehicles, one has to either scratch build or modify an existing kit or donor RTR model.

The conversion project outlined here describes the creation of a 13T short-wheel base (9ft wheelbase) brake van, converted from a Ratio 20T Brake Van kit. I used the prototype illustrated in Russell (1971: fig. 243) and the respective line-drawing (Russell 1971: 135), as the principal source of research information. The purpose of this project was to see if it was possible to produce a reasonable representation of this particular prototype in 4mm scale using relatively inexpensive, commercially available, plastic kits as the starting point.

LIST OF MATERIALS REQUIRED

The following kits and components were assembled prior to any work commencing on the conversion project:

- Ratio GWR 20T Brake Van kit (ref: 569)
- Cooper Craft GWR 9ft wheelbase kit (ref: 1012)
- Gibson eight-spoke wheels and brass bearings
- Couplings of choice – I used Bachmann couplings (ref: 36-025)
- Replacement white metal buffers (ABS GWR standard fitted wagon buffers)
- Replacement white metal RCH coupling hooks (ABS or similar)
- Additional steel ballast wagon weights (Cooper Craft)
- 0.5mm wire for axle box tie bars
- GWR wagon grey paint (for the body and underframe)
- Humbrol matt white paint (for the roof)
- HMRS Pressfix transfers

The parts from the Ratio Brake Van kit and the Cooper Craft underframe kit were examined and the appropriate parts removed from the kits necessary

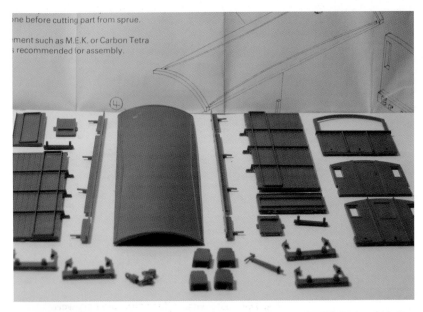

Fig. 161 *The starting point of this project is the standard brake van kit and instructions.*

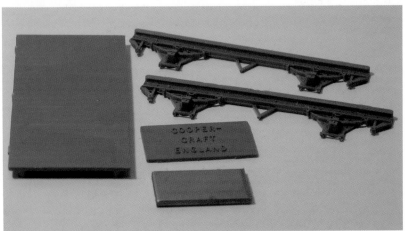

Fig. 162 *The shorter version of the brake van had a wheelbase of 9ft. A 9ft wheelbase Cooper Craft kit was used as the basis for the new underframe.*

Fig. 163 In addition to the standard kit parts, replacement wheels, brass bearings, buffers, coupling hooks and tension link couplings were required.

to complete this project, as detailed above. The remaining parts were put in the spares' box for use on future projects.

The following items were taken from the Ratio GWR 20T Brake Van kit:

- Roof, sides, ends, internal wall
- Sand boxes
- Running boards and access steps
- Hand brake, brake gear, lamps

The following items taken from Cooper Craft kit:

- Floor
- Sole-bars and axle boxes (although not exactly the correct pattern, I decided they were close enough for this purpose) with 'V' hangers removed from sole bars

CONSTRUCTION OF THE UNDERFRAME

The underframe kit was assembled in the normal way, except that the 'V' hangars were removed from each sole bar before construction began. Brass bearings were installed in the axle boxes before fixing to the floor and then the sole bars fixed to the underside of the floor. The wheel sets were installed at this stage to check alignment and that they were free-running.

Fig. 164 The wagon floor and sole bars were modified by comparing the kit parts to 4mm scale line-drawings of the prototype and cutting as appropriate.

A 1mm diameter hole was drilled in the veranda end of the floor at this stage to accommodate the hand-brake stanchion after the body had been completed. A ballast weight was added to the floor recess, as is normal with Cooper Craft kits, and a further two wagon weights were glued together and then fixed to the floor directly above the recess to provide additional ballast, these being hidden within the van body of the finished model.

Fig. 165 The underframe was then constructed as per the standard kit instructions and replacement wheels added.

The running boards from the brake van kit had to be shortened to match the length of the new wagon. I have described the process of modification here as they form part of the chassis, but when building the model I found it easier to construct the body first, then return to fit the running boards and axle tie bars.

I found that starting at one end of the running board, the existing cut-out for the axle box can be located over one axle box. The overall length of the running board can then be marked, as well as the location for the second cut-out. The running board was shortened and shaped at each end to match the prototype.

The second axle box cut-out was formed by scoring the back of the vertical component with a sharp knife and then scoring along the joint with the horizontal section between the two vertical

Fig. 166 The running boards were modified by shortening and cutting new slots to sit over the axle boxes. New fixing points are shown as white pieces of plasticard microstrip cut to fit and fixed to the underframe, as appropriate.

Fig. 167   The modified brake van with new running boards attached and showing how they need to sit squarely over the axle boxes.

cuts. This small piece can then be removed and the horizontal section carefully filed with a small square-section file to the correct depth to sit squarely over the axle box. This was a slow repetitive process as the plastic part is fragile and can be broken if the cutting and filing is too vigorous!

To fix the running board to the side frames, vertical brackets are provided on the brake van kit and these had to be replicated on the modified wagon. To achieve this, vertical strips were added to the sole bar at the locations to match the fixing brackets on the running board. To get these strips in the correct locations, the modified running board was offered up to the sole bar and marked at the three locations of the fixing brackets. Representative 'bracket' fixings were then formed using microstrip plasticard to the correct length, shown as small white sections in the accompanying photographs (see Fig. 166). The running boards were then fixed to the strips and the axle boxes as per the normal way following the kit instructions.

The photograph of the prototype showed that the axle boxes on each side were connected with a tie bar. This is not present as part of the 9ft wheelbase underframe kit, so I used some 0.5mm diameter wire cut to length and super-glued to each axle box to represent this part of the wagon, as shown in Fig. 168.

Below the door on each side of the veranda, the brake van kit has an access step part that fixes to the sole bar. I found that these needed some minor modification of the vertical strips to fit in the sole bar, as shown in Fig. 167.

CONSTRUCTION OF THE WAGON BODY

Examination of the position of the floor in the underframe kit, compared to that in the brake van kit, indicated that the floor level was slightly higher and thus the sidewalls had to be modified internally to fit around the underframe floor. This required the removal of the lip on the internal sides of the walls that are used to locate the walls correctly to the floor/sole bar components of the brake van kit, as shown in Fig. 169.

The first decision to be made in the construction of the body shell was whether to retain the moulded hand rails, as provided on the brake van kit, or to remove and replace them with fine wire. The vertical bracing on the sides was to be retained, so this would require at least four cuts in the sidewalls to reduce the length of the wall. On this basis I opted to retain the moulded hand rails as otherwise this would further complicate the modification process and weaken the walls of the final model.

Fig. 168   In this side view of a modified van, the axle box tie rods formed from 0.5mm diameter wire have been added and fixed in place with cyanoacrylate adhesive.

Fig. 169   The use of the Cooper Craft underframe and wagon floor required internal modification of the sidewalls to remove the floor lip so that it would sit flush on the new floor.

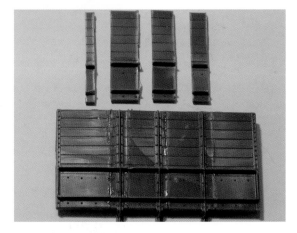

Fig. 170   The sidewall was marked after laying on a line-drawing of the prototype. The walls were cut and then re-assembled in the shortened form, with the discarded wall sections shown above.

Scaling the dimensions from the line-drawings, the walls were marked with cut lines at the appropriate locations. The cuts were made by scoring each line with a sharp craft knife on the external surface and then cutting the internal wall surface. The vertical joints were subsequently cleaned up with a fine file and the sidewalls reassembled in the correct order in the shortened form to represent the modified wagon.

Using a piece of scrap plastic sprue, I formed a bracing bar to strengthen the walls and this was fixed along the internal face of the walls towards the upper edge, as shown in Fig. 172, of the partially completed body; the joint with the floor providing the bracing at the lower edge of the walls.

The van end wall of the wagon and the veranda end wall can be used unaltered from the kit, as well

Fig. 171 A comparison of original and shortened sidewalls gives an indication of the reduced length of the modified wagon.

Fig. 172 Plastic wagon kits are light and require ballasting to improve running, even more so for a brake van at the end of a train. In this internal view of the wagon under construction, additional ballast weights and wall bracing can be seen.

as the access half-door/gate to each side of the veranda. The sidewalls of the veranda were modified in the same way as the sidewalls of the van section. I opted to retain the moulded hand rails and removed a central portion of the wall by making two vertical cuts and then fixing the two ends back together to form the shortened wall, as shown in Figs 173 and 174.

The internal end wall of the van section had to be modified to remove a small amount from the base of the wall to fit with the floor of the underframe kit and this modification should be undertaken once the sidewalls have been fixed in place so that the piece can be marked to match the sidewalls.

Construction of the body began with the van end wall and then the two sidewalls. Once happy that

Fig. 173 A close-up of the shortened veranda wall shows how the handrail detail was retained and carefully cut.

Fig. 174 A view of a veranda under construction showing how the parts fit together along the new wagon floor.

Fig. 175 The internal wall of the van body had to be modified to fit on top of the wagon floor and retain the correct roof line.

Fig. 176 The replacement buffers and coupling hook were added to the veranda end wall before fixing to the wagon body.

these were square and vertical, the internal van wall was checked and trimmed to fit accordingly, as per the brake van kit instructions. I found it useful to insert a small piece of scrap plastic bar at the mid-point of the van section to ensure that the walls

Fig. 177 After completion of all of the modifications to the bodywork, the van was ready for painting.

remained vertical and to prevent later risk of bowing of the sidewalls, as shown in Fig. 177.

Once the van section was completed, the veranda doors and sidewall were then fixed in position and, finally, the veranda end wall, as shown in Fig. 177. I would like to add a note of caution here when utilizing the veranda end wall and frame. The frame for the upper section of the veranda end is extremely fragile and easily broken, as I found to my cost, whilst carrying out this project. From my experience, it is best to leave this part of the body off whilst all of the rest of the upper bodywork is completed and the running boards, steps and wire tie bars for the axle boxes added, so as to reduce the risk of damage. Once all is complete, then add the end wall and after this has been fixed in place, add the sand boxes and hand brake stanchion.

MODIFICATION OF THE ROOF

The final major piece of work was the modification of the roof to meet the dimensions for the new wagon. The roof from the brake van kit needed shortening and modifying. Specifically, the incorrect chimney, as moulded on the kit roof, needed to be removed and a new chimney added in the correct location, as shown on the line-drawings and the images from which I worked. The chimney was carefully removed with a sharp knife and the roof smoothed with a fine

file. A piece of scrap plastic was shaped and cleaned up for use as a new chimney.

I would recommend that the roof is not cut until after the body has been constructed, so that the measurements can be made from the completed model. Two cut lines were marked on the underside of the roof by measuring the distance between the internal edges of the two end walls, so that the overlap arrangement of the roof is retained at each end of the wagon. The central section of the roof was removed and the two ends re-joined and the joint flooded with liquid polystyrene cement. The roof was then placed on a flat (glass tile) surface to harden off before being gently sanded to blend the joint line, as shown in Fig. 178. The new chimney was added on the roof centre-line and positioned such that it was between the central vertical bracing strips on the sidewalls, as shown in the line-drawings.

FINISHING TOUCHES

The body was painted GWR wagon dark grey and the roof matt white and then lightly weathered to give an 'in service look' rather than a fresh out of the paint shops look. Once the paintwork on the sidewalls was dry, windows were cut from clear plastic sheet and glued, using PVA, to the external rebate of the window openings in each end

Fig. 178   The roof was shortened similar to that described previously for vans and then test-fitted to the body.

Fig. 179   The wagon was painted in GWR wagon grey and the roof painted white to represent a newly completed wagon. In service the roof would have quickly discoloured to grey or even black.

Fig. 180 On this model the decals added are to the correct style as the prototype, but the depot name is the modeller's licence to allow the wagon to be accommodated on the author's layout.

of the van section walls. PVA was used here as it dries clear, so any excess glue does not unduly detract from a clear window finish on the model. The hand rails were picked out in white using a fine brush. Once the paintwork was completed, the roof was then added to the body and Pressfix transfers applied.

It should be noted that the allocation to 'Bala' shown on the brake van is purely fictitious, as it is for use on my layout, rather than as a historically accurate model.

Depending on your personal preference of couplings, these can be added during the construction of the wagon or when it is completed. I use tension lock couplings on my layout and, therefore, fitted Bachmann small couplings, fixed to the tension lock coupling mounting block supplied in the Cooper Craft kit.

CONVERSION 5: CREATION OF A GWR SIX-WHEEL HEAVY BRAKE VAN

BACKGROUND

This conversion project describes the creation of a 13ft wheelbase 24T brake van, which, similar to the

conversion described in Conversion 4, was achieved utilizing a Ratio 20T Brake Van kit. Prototype research identified good photographs of this wagon in service, as illustrated in Russell (1971: figs 247 and 248), and the respective line-drawing (Russell 1971: 135) provided useful dimensional information for the project.

The purpose of this exercise was to see if it was possible to produce a reasonable representation of this particular prototype in 4mm scale using a relatively inexpensive, commercially available, plastic kit as the starting point. This conversion records my attempts, together with a series of photographs, to provide some hints as to how the model was completed.

LIST OF MATERIALS REQUIRED

The following kits and component parts, as shown in Fig. 182, should be sourced prior to commencing the conversion project:

- Ratio GWR 20T Brake Van kit (5069)
- Gibson wheels and brass bearings (outer axles)
- Plastic wagon wheel axle from spares' box for central axle
- Additional axle boxes and springs from previous project – I used ones to the same pattern

Fig. 181   *At the opposite end of the scale to the previous example, this model is of one of the six-wheel variety heavy brake vans.*

as the prototype, kept as spares from a Parkside cattle van kit
- Additional brake shoes cut from spare wagon brake gear, then bent to shape
- Couplings of choice – I used Bachmann couplings (36-025)

- ABS wagon buffers – I used GWR standard fitted wagon pattern buffers
- ABS RCH coupling hooks
- ABS hanging-type vacuum pipes
- Additional ballast (Cooper Craft wagon weights and nails)

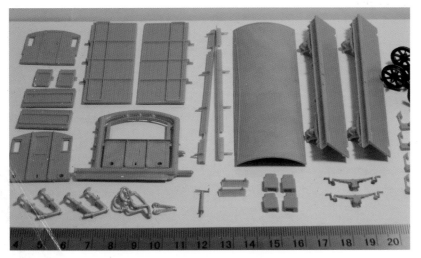

Fig. 182   *The basic kit's parts required, but also the replacement components required, as well as the additional central axle boxes and springs to a different pattern from the outer ones.*

- Plasticard microstrip (various sizes) to form central axle 'W' irons, step hangers and other minor modifications to the body, as described in the text
- 0.5mm wire for axle box tie bars (optional)
- GWR wagon grey paint (for the body and underframe)
- Humbrol matt white paint (for the roof)
- HMRS Pressfix transfers

CONSTRUCTION OF THE UNDERFRAME

The length of the six-wheel Toad was approximately 20ft, about 4ft shorter that the four-wheel 20T version on which the Ratio kit is based. Therefore, the underframe had to be shortened to match the prototype, while retaining a scale 13ft between the two outer axles. To accomplish this, I found it best to join the two halves of the underframe/floor section of the kit together, as shown in the kit instructions, and then mark and cut to length. Prior to cutting the floor, the plastic tie bar and the central hanging points for the running board were removed from each side of the assembly and put aside for re-use.

Once the joined halves had hardened off, I marked up the correct length of underframe by measuring the same length in from each end and marking two cut lines for the removal of the central section of the floor, as shown in Figs 183 and 184. The underframe was subsequently cut using a fine-tooth razor saw and the two ends cleaned up and re-joined.

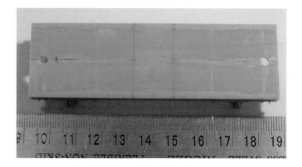

Fig. 184 The floor of the standard kit was too long for the wagon being modelled when compared to the line-drawings. The floor was subsequently fixed together and cut lines marked for shortening.

When the modified floor section was set, brass bearings were installed in the two outer axle boxes and the wheel sets installed to check alignment and that they were free-running. The additional central axle boxes/springs were then fixed to the sole bars to match the layout shown on the prototype. These additional axle boxes/springs were derived from my spares' box and I believe came from a Parkside Beetle kit. They have the same visual appearance as the prototype, but have no 'W' irons. I therefore used microstrip to form the 'W' to match the line-drawings, as shown by the white plastic pieces in Figs 185, 186 and 187. Once these details had been completed, the central axle was installed and checked for alignment and free-running.

Fig. 183 A close-up of the additional central axle box and spring showing the difference to the standard arrangement.

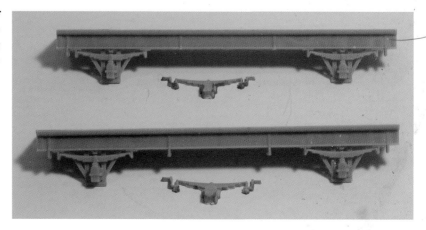

Fig. 185 The shorted chassis reassembled and central axle box added to show wheel arrangement.

Fig. 186 A representation of the 'W' irons for central axle and tie rods was fabricated from plasticard microstrip.

Fig. 187 An underside view of the wagon to show the detail of the axle configuration.

Fig. 188   Additional steel ballast weights were added on the underside of the floor above each axle to improve adhesion to the track.

Fig. 189   The completed underframe after modifications and testing to ensure that the three axle arrangement could negotiate layout curves and points.

The choice of wheel set for the central axle had to take account of the need for lateral movement on curved track and points. Whilst there are all kinds of technical solutions to this problem, I was looking to achieve something simple. I used Alan Gibson fine-scale pin-point wheel sets, with brass bearings inserted in the axle boxes on the outer axles, but set to allow some slight lateral movement on each axle (approximately 1mm either way).

For the centre axle, I omitted the brass bearings from the axle boxes and used a plastic wheel set from my spares' box (uncertain origin),

suitably cleaned up and fine sanded so that the pin-point axle ends were able to move side to side and up and down within the axle box, thus providing lateral and vertical movement on curves. Not a very technical solution, but this seems to have worked well on my layout and the main layout at the local club.

Ballast weights (Cooper Craft) were added to the underside of the wagon floor above each axle as shown in Fig. 188. The brake shoes for each wheel were then added and I found that due to the presence of the ballast weights, the brake gear parts supplied with the kit had to be cut into individual brake shoe components and glued separately, either side of each wheel. Brake shoes for the central axle were formed from parts cut from spare wagon brake gear sets, suitably bent to shape. The advantage of fixing the brake shoes in this manner was that they could be glued in position with the wheels in place and so ensured that they were correctly aligned and checked as the work proceeded.

The running boards from the brake van kit had to be shortened to match the length of the new wagon. Careful study of the prototype photographs and line-drawing showed that each running board was held in place by three hanging points: two below the van end and one at the veranda end of the wagon. I found that, starting at the van end of the wagon, the running board could be lined up with the outer axle and was marked and cut at the mid-point of the central axle.

A second hanging point was formed from micro-strip plasticard at the appropriate location to match the prototype. The section of running board was then modified to provide the 'cut-out' around the centre axle. The process was then repeated starting at the opposite end of the wagon, so that the join in the running board was at the mid-point of the central axle. The running boards were then fixed to the hanging points and axle boxes as per the normal way following the kit instructions, as shown in Figs 195 and 196.

The photograph of the prototype showed that the axle boxes were connected with a tie bar. So I carefully cut the plastic tie bar (removed from the kit at the beginning) to the correct length and fixed it, as shown in Fig. 187. This part is very fine and prone to breaking, therefore, if preferred one could use 0.5mm diameter wire cut to length and super-glued to each axle box.

A 1mm diameter hole was drilled in the veranda end of the floor at this stage to accommodate the hand-brake stanchion after the body had been completed, as shown in Fig. 184. The larger holes in the floor of the kit, intended to take the support for the PECO-style coupling were also filled with spare bits of plasticard at the same time.

CONSTRUCTION OF THE WAGON BODY

The first decision to be made in the construction of the body shell was whether to retain the moulded hand rails, as provided on the brake van kit, or to remove and replace them with fine wire. As I had decided to retain the vertical bracing on the sides, this would require at least four vertical cuts in the sidewalls to reduce the overall length. On this basis I opted to retain the moulded hand rails, as otherwise this would further complicate the modification process and weaken the walls of the final model.

Scaling the relevant dimensions from the line-drawings, the walls were marked with cut lines at the appropriate locations, which resulted in removing 2mm from each end section and 1mm from each of the two inner sections of each side, as shown in Figs 190 and 191. The cuts were made by scoring each line with a sharp craft knife on the external surface and then cutting the internal wall surface with a sharp craft knife. The vertical joints were subsequently cleaned up with a fine file and the sidewalls re-assembled in the correct order in the shortened form to represent the modified wagon, as shown in the photographs.

Fig. 190   Modification of the sidewall was required as for the previous example. Cut lines were marked on the internal face of the walls and a sharp craft knife was used to carefully score and cut the plastic body.

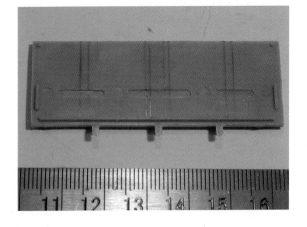

Using a piece of scrap 2mm-thick plastic card (in my case off-cuts from a Wills embossed plasticard sheet), I formed a bracing bar to strengthen the walls and this was fixed along the internal face of the walls towards the upper edge, as shown in Fig. 193; the joint with the floor provided the bracing at the lower edge of the walls.

The van end wall of the wagon, the internal partition wall and the veranda end wall can all be used unaltered from the kit (as seen in Fig. 192), as well as the access half-door/gate to each side of the veranda. The sidewalls of the veranda were modified in the same way as the sidewalls of the van section. I opted to retain the moulded hand rails and removed a central portion of the wall by making two vertical cuts and removing a section about 7mm in length from each side. The two ends were then glued back together to form the shortened wall, as shown in Fig. 194.

Fig. 191   After re-assembly of the modified sidewall a comparison of original and shortened sidewall shows the small reduction in length.

Fig. 192   The end walls were modified with replacement white metal buffers and coupling hooks. Care needs to be taken with the veranda end as the arch is extremely fragile and easily broken.

Fig. 193   Brake van assembly almost complete, showing the inclusion of internal bracing on the sidewalls using scrap plastic sheet and sprue to prevent bowing.

Fig. 194 A close-up view of the veranda modifications showing the detail retained and the installation of the top step on the sole bar.

Construction of the body began with the van end wall and then the two sidewalls. Once happy that these were square and vertical, the van partition wall was then glued in position as per the brake van kit instructions. I found it useful to insert a small piece of scrap plastic bar at the mid-point of the van section to ensure that the walls remained vertical and to prevent later risk of bowing of the sidewalls, as shown in Fig. 193.

Once the van section was completed, the veranda doors and sidewall were then fixed in position and then finally the veranda end wall. After the end wall

was fixed in place, the sand boxes and hand-brake stanchion were added. Further ballast, for which I used steel nails cut to length, was subsequently glued to the floor inside the van end of the wagon to add more weight, before the roof was added.

MODIFICATION OF THE ROOF

The final major piece of work is the modification of the roof to meet the dimensions for the new wagon. The roof from the brake van kit needed shortening and the chimney modifying. The incorrect chimney moulding was removed and a new chimney added in the correct location, as shown on the line-drawings and the images from which I worked. The chimney was carefully removed with a sharp knife and the roof smoothed with a fine file. A piece of scrap plastic was shaped for use as a new chimney.

I would recommend that the roof is not cut until after the body has been constructed, so that the measurements can be made from the completed model. Once the body had been completed, the internal measurement between the end walls was found to be 78mm. Two cut lines were marked on the underside of the roof by measuring the distance between the internal edges of the two end walls, so that the overlap arrangement of the roof was retained at each end of the wagon.

Fig. 195 The running boards were modified by retaining one of the original cut outs at each end and then marking and cutting two new cut outs for the other axles.

Fig. 196   The roof was shortened by removing a section from the centre to retain the rain-strip detail. A new chimney formed from waste plastic sprue was added in the correct location.

The central section of the roof was removed and the two ends re-joined and the joint flooded with liquid polystyrene cement. The roof was then placed on a flat (glass tile) surface to harden off before being gently sanded to blend the joint line. The new chimney was added on the roof centre-line and between the first and second vertical bracing strips on the sidewalls, starting at the van end, as shown in the line-drawings.

FINISHING TOUCHES

The body was painted GWR wagon dark grey and the roof matt white and then lightly weathered to give an 'in service look' rather than a fresh out of the paint shops look. Once the paintwork on the sidewalls was dry, windows were cut from clear plastic sheet and glued, using PVA (that dries clear), to the external rebate of the window openings in each end of the van section walls. The hand rails were picked out in white using a fine brush. Once the paintwork was completed, the roof was then glued to the body and finally Pressfix transfers applied, as shown in Figs 197 and 198.

Tail lamps and side lamps can be added, according to preference, and on this particular model I also added vacuum pipes, painted red to signify through

Fig. 197   Brake vans were not generally vacuum braked vehicles. However, in this example a capacity to provide through vacuum braking from the locomotive was catered for and the pipe work was clearly identified by being painted red.

Fig. 198 The finished model painted and identified as a Wolverhampton depot vehicle from the decals.

piping as described in Mr Russell's book (1971), as I understand that Toads were not fitted with vacuum cylinders as a rule, just the piping and a brake setter handle being provided.

LESSONS LEARNED

As you will have gathered from some of the points noted in both this conversion and the previous example for the short wheelbased vehicle, there were a number of useful lessons learned, things that may be of use should you want to replicate these kit conversions:

1. The veranda end wall and frame is extremely fragile and easily broken; fix this to the wagon as the last item before adding the roof
2. Adding the windows using clear drying PVA can be done after all of the paintwork has been completed
3. Mark and cut the roof after the body has been constructed to get exact measurements
4. As with any kit construction, dry runs before fixing are essential and particularly where you have modified parts from their original form and there are no instructions to follow
5. The running board components are also very fragile parts and this fact needs to be borne in mind when modifying them, as

described above; patience is the key – do it a bit at a time

CONVERSION OF READY-TO-RUN ROLLING STOCK

The previous conversions in this chapter have shown what can be achieved by a number of conversion projects using commercially available kits as the starting point. Although this book is focused on the building of kits and scratch building, I thought that it might also be useful to include a quick look at what can be achieved from converting RTR rolling stock as an alternative to using kits as the donor parts for your project. The following worked example is based on a short article (Tisdale 2012b), which I have extended and provided with further details; it describes how I attempted to create a non-standard version of a GWR brake van, or Toad, through modification of a RTR model.

The inspiration for this transformation project came from the desire to create something a bit different to run on my layout *Llanfair*; to create a version of a brake van that was not the 'standard' GWR Toad. Reference to Russell (1971: 119–120) indicated a non-standard GWR prototype with a Welsh flavour, perfect for my layout. Initially, I contemplated scratch building, but having spotted

Fig. 199   At the time of Grouping in 1923, the GWR absorbed a number of pieces of rolling stock from various smaller railway companies. This example is a representation of a Cambrian Railway's brake van.

a Bachmann 20T BR Brake Van model on the sale stand at the Jersey Model Railway Club Exhibition I thought that this might be a good place to start. The following notes and accompanying photographs describe my attempt at the conversion of the 20T BR Brake Van into an alternative GWR Toad brake van.

LIST OF MATERIALS REQUIRED

Before describing the approach that I took, it might be useful to summarize the materials that I used, should you wish to consider trying the same process:

- The starting point was a Bachmann BR 20T standard brake van model (ref: 33-803); these models are currently out of production, but I picked my example up for £5 at an exhibition sale stand, or one can be sourced second-hand via the internet
- Coupling hooks – I used ABS white metal ones from my stock of parts in the modelling box

- Approximately 180mm of 0.45mm diameter (or similar) fine wire for use as the replacement long hand rails on each side of the van body
- A few large (No.56) staples, or similar, to form the grab rails on each side of the doors, the horizontal handrail on each door and the central supports to the lower footsteps
- Assorted pieces of 0.5mm (20thou) plasticard and plastic microstrip
- Tail lamps for the finished model
- Guard figure for the veranda – I used a Dart Castings figure of a guard leaning out and watching the world go by
- Paint and transfers of preference

The first step was to remove the body from the chassis. This was achieved by removing the screw on the underside of the model and gently prising apart the four lugs that hold the body to the chassis.

Fig. 200   A model of the Cambrian Railway brake van has been created from a conversion of a RTR BR 20T standard brake van model made by Bachmann.

Fig. 201   The body is removed from the chassis by unscrewing the locating screw on the underside of the wagon and then gently easing the retaining lugs clear of the underframe.

The screw should be put somewhere safe for re-use when the conversion work has been completed.

The modification process can be divided into two distinct sections of work: first, the work required on the body and roof; and, second, the work required on the chassis. I have divided these notes up on this basis.

WORK REQUIRED TO THE BODY AND ROOF

Once removed from the chassis, the first part of the process was to compare the model against the photograph of the prototype and to determine what needed to be changed to achieve the transformation. Removal of the guard's lookout duckets on each side of the van body and the removal of the existing moulded hand rails were the most obvious requirements in respect of the body sides; whilst on the roof, the rain-strips, ventilators and chimney all needed to be removed.

Starting with the roof, the chimney was removed carefully with a sharp chisel blade knife flush to the roof surface and retained for re-use on the modified model. The moulded ventilator and rain-strip protrusions were then removed using fine files and fine-grade glass paper until a smooth roof profile was

Fig. 202   The moulded detail on the roof of the donor wagon for rain-strips above each doorway and chimney roof detail was carefully removed with a sharp craft knife and fine-grade sandpaper.

Fig. 204   The modified areas on the sidewalls were subsequently scribed using a craft knife to provide a representation of planking to match the remainder of the wagon body.

Fig. 203   The handrails and guard duckets were also removed from the RTR wagon.

obtained, as shown in Fig. 202. Once I was happy with the roof profile, new rain-strips were added to each end of the roof using plastic microstrip.

Along each side of the roof, I marked out the arc of the rain-strip using a pencil line and a suitably sized tin lid. As with the ends of the roof, plastic microstrip was then used to form these rain-strips along the marked lines, which were fixed in place with liquid polystyrene cement. The original chimney salvaged from the model was then re-located at the mid-point along one side of the wagon between the rain-strip and the roof edge, as per the prototype.

This completed the work required to the roof prior to painting.

On the body sides, the guard's duckets were removed with a fine razor saw, followed by sanding with glass paper and then the use of fine files to remove the profile of this protrusion on the body. Fortunately, on the Bachmann model, the body side at the location of the duckets is a solid, thickened section of the wall, rather than a moulded extruded section, thus removing the ducket did not reveal a hole in the wall that would require filling as I had originally feared.

After dealing with the duckets, the moulded hand rails were removed with a fine file and the smooth areas where the numbers and lettering were located on the model were lightly sanded to remove these transfers and roughen the surface slightly. Once each side of the body had been treated as described above, I then used a sharp craft knife, steel rule and fine razor saw to re-scribe the vertical planking over the modified areas to match the existing planking. It should be noted here that the prototype had wider and thus fewer vertical planks than that reproduced on the model. I contemplated sanding the sides completely flush and scribing the correct plank widths, but in this instance decided to accept the incorrect planking pattern as a compromise, to reduce the amount of work required.

Fig. 205 Microstrip and plasticard sheet modifications are shown in white, comprising doors, new chimney, rain-strips to the roof and angle-iron bracing to the sidewalls.

Fig. 206 The end wall modifications included the addition of plastic microstrip bracing detail and cosmetic coupling hooks. Hand rails were added using staples and fine wire.

The next stage of the process was to re-create the vertical bracing of the prototype on the model. On each side of the body, bracing was added to sub-divide the wall into three sections, with the central section slightly narrower than each end section. Plastic microstrip was used to create the 'T' section bracing, as shown in Figs 205 and 206. If preferred, one could use a pre-formed plastic 'T' section or etched brass bracing strip as an alternative to the plastic microstrip.

Doors were then added to each of the openings at each veranda end of the wagon. A piece of 0.5mm thickness (20thou) plasticard was cut approximately 10mm wide to match the width of the opening and 11mm high to match the profile of the end walls. Each 'door' was scribed with vertical planking to match the body walls and thin strips added on each vertical front edge to represent the recessed door. Plastic microstrip was then used to create the overhanging top edge beam across the doorways and open veranda ends, as per the prototype and as shown in the accompanying photographs.

This completed the work to the body prior to reassembly with the chassis. The bracing on the end walls had to be added once the model was re-assembled, as the bracing continues down to the level of the coupling hook on the buffer beam, to match that shown on the prototype.

WORK REQUIRED TO THE CHASSIS

The main area of difference between the model and the prototype was the side steps. On the production model there were two steps on each side, extending the full length of the body. However, on the prototype, there was a lower step extending the full length and two shorter upper steps at each end where the access doors were located. As the detail on the model was all one moulding, work to modify the steps had to be undertaken carefully.

The main requirement was to remove approximately two-thirds of the length of the upper step from the moulding and the central support for the steps. I started with a sharp knife to mark the position of the cut lines and then used a fine razor saw to remove the central section of the upper step between the axle springs. This was the relatively easy part.

The next step was to work on the section of upper step that extends across the front of the axle springs, to a point approximately above the centre-line of the axle boxes. This section was removed, a small piece at a time, using a combination of sharp craft knife and a selection of grinding tool bits on my mini-drill and fine files to smooth off the cut surface.

As you can see from the photographs taken during this stage, I chose not to completely remove the step

Fig. 207   The chassis of the RTR model was generally left untouched, except for the removal of the upper running board.

Fig. 208   An additional central support to the lower running board was formed from a staple suitably cut and bent to shape.

all the way back to the front face of the axle spring. Instead, I decided to stop once I had removed the step back far enough to reveal the vertical support that was present on the inner edge of the axle spring, so that the chassis moulding wasn't weakened. Once this had been smoothed and painted I was satisfied that this was a reasonable compromise in terms of the overall impression.

When the removal of the parts described above was completed, I then used a couple of large staples, suitably cut and bent to shape, to create the 'new' vertical supports to the lower step, located at the mid-point of each side, as per the prototype. Thin pieces of microstrip were then cut and glued in place to fill the gaps in the lower step across the front of each axle box, to match the prototype.

On each end of the chassis, I chose to retain the tension lock couplings and mounting blocks as supplied, as well as the moulded buffers, although the latter were cleaned up using a fine file to remove the flash and mould lines. If preferred, the couplings could be unscrewed, mounting blocks removed and replaced with couplings of preference. In addition, the moulded buffers could also be removed and replaced with more prototypical examples. Coupling hooks were super-glued to the buffer beam, as shown in the photographs.

The modified body and chassis were then reassembled and the two sets of vertical bracing on each end wall were added. These sections of bracing were formed from microstrip in the same way as described above for the sidewalls. As noted above, this bracing extends from the top of the veranda wall to the bottom of the buffer beam, across the joint between body and chassis and can only be added once the body and chassis are joined together.

For the hand rails, I used large staples to form the short horizontal handle on each door and the vertical grab rails on each side of each door. The two long horizontal hand rails on each side were formed using 0.45mm diameter wire. All of the hand rails were fixed with super glue and small pieces of microstrip were used at each end of the horizontal hand rails to represent the fixing points. This work completed the addition of new detail prior to painting. I chose to retain the three-hole disc wheels as supplied on the Bachmann model, but if preferred these could be changed to spoked wheels.

Fig. 209 The fully modified van re-assembled prior to the application of paint and decals.

The body and chassis were painted all over Great Western wagon grey, except the roof and hand rails, which were painted white, as per early 1930s practice and which fits with the time period of my layout. HMRS Pressfix transfers were then used to reproduce the lettering and numbering. The final touches to the model included the addition of tail lamps and a guard figure leaning out over the veranda, for which I used the figure produced by Dart Castings.

I found that the transformation process required a series of compromises to be made in terms of prototypical detail to achieve the overall goal. As I have pointed out above, a number of deviations from the prototype detail have been accepted in producing this model, but the aim was to demonstrate that it is possible to produce a piece of distinctive rolling stock relatively easily from a commercially produced RTR model without necessarily resorting to a complete scratch build.

I am pleased with the result achieved and hope this has inspired others to try. I accept that purists will point out the errors in the model produced and for this apologize; however, I did not set out to produce a 100 per cent accurate reproduction of the prototype in 4mm scale.

Fig. 210 The wagon was painted in the standard GWR colour scheme, with hand rails picked out in white. The decals indicate a Towyn-based vehicle. The R.U. designation signifies that it was restricted to operating within the Towyn locality.

CHAPTER SIX

SCRATCH BUILDING WAGONS AND VANS

WHY SCRATCH BUILD WAGONS AND VANS?

This is a common question, as I have already discussed in Chapter 1, especially when you consider the wide variety of models and kits available to the railway modeller from the industry today. However, no matter what the range of RTR and/or kit wagons on offer, there is always going to be a specific prototype variation or special wagon that a modeller would like, which is not covered by the range of kits and RTR wagons on offer. The more specialized or obscure the prototype requirement, the greater the likelihood is that there will not be a model readily available, as the market will be so small as to not make it financially viable to produce a RTR model or commercial kit.

Scratch building can, therefore, be considered as the next logical step after kit conversion or RTR conversion, in that search for modelling something that little bit different. The driver to move down this route will be the desire to create a specific prototype or less widely modelled version of a more common prototype. At some point you will need to decide what you think you are able and can achieve through conversion of a kit or RTR model. You need to recognize that beyond that point it is likely to be more efficient and easier to achieve the model that you wish to create by starting completely from scratch.

This decision will partially be guided by the level of confidence that you have in your ability as a modeller to either build from scratch, or use an existing kit, or RTR model, as the basis for the project in hand. The time to undertake the work, the degree of accuracy you want to achieve and how much you will need to or, perhaps more importantly, be willing to compromise, also need to be considered in the decision-making process.

To scratch build a wagon or van, will very likely take you more time than if you were putting together a kit, or converting a RTR model. But the opportunity is there for you to create a model with fewer compromises having to be accepted; it will also allow you to produce something that may be unique to your prototype era/region/operation, and these may be the deciding factors. It is also linked to your confidence in your level of skill and ability as a modeller, but without giving it a go you will not know whether it is within your grasp or not.

SELECTING THE PROTOTYPE

Selecting the prototype that you want to model as a particular project will depend on your own personal preferences – there is no one reason for considering scratch building. Some will decide to go this route because the particular prototype is not available in RTR or kit form. Others may decide to go down this path to create a model of a prototype that is to a higher level of accuracy than that available from a RTR model or commercially available kit. Another reason is to create a wagon that is specific to a particular period or subject matter. The decision-making process guiding the selection of your prototype as the subject of a scratch building project is, therefore, subject to numerous variables and no two situations are likely to be the same.

In my case, it was the desire to create some examples of rolling stock that were not readily available as kits or RTR models. I chose to model particular prototypes because either they fitted with the period and location that I was trying to create on my layout, or I wanted to have something just that little bit different. These tend to be the overriding motives behind getting me started on scratch building rolling stock.

Having made the decision to want to model something a bit different, I then spend many hours browsing through my collection of books, journals and magazines, as well as sources of information

Fig. 211   *Scratch building wagons allows you to build something that may not be available RTR or in kit form. This example of a scratch built GWR gas tank wagon was a first attempt at scratch building.*

on the internet to see what would take my eye. There is no particular formula to this process – it is largely governed by whatever catches my attention during the review of the sources of information. For example, the first piece of scratch building that I attempted, in terms of railway rolling stock, was the creation of the GWR Cordon Gas Tank wagon, about which I subsequently wrote a short article that was published in *Railway Modeller* (Tisdale 2010a). An expanded and more detailed description of the construction of this scratch built wagon has been included in Chapter 7 for reference.

RESEARCH

Once your subject matter has been selected, the next step is to undertake research, to obtain as much information as you think necessary to enable you to build the model of the prototype. As with the selection process, the amount of research you choose to do is down to personal preference – there is no right or wrong answer as to how much is correct.

On the basis of my experience, my advice would be that research is the key to the process and is highly recommended as a 'must do' activity before starting any project of this type. The more information that you collect, the better – there is no such thing as too much information. The basic requirement will depend on the subject matter being tackled, but the key elements are a scaled line-drawing for dimensions and photographs of the completed prototype wagon as the built wagons often did not adhere to the line-drawing in practice. Ideally, the photographs should date from the time period that you wish to model it, as changes to wagons were made during maintenance and adaptations occurred over the years in service to meet the requirements of the time.

The more photographs available of different sides, angles and close-up of key details, such as brake gear and underframe, the better but is not essential. I have found that in many cases good photographic records can be found for the newly built and out-shopped wagon, but trying to model a prototype in service does tend to require more filtering through dozens of photographs of passing goods trains, goods yard shots and sidings to identify what a particular wagon looked like in day to day operation on the real railway.

As I am reviewing the text and photographs of the selected subject, I find it useful to make notes on the shapes of key elements of the structure of the wagon and, where possible, I also try to estimate dimensions of the wagon or particular features of the wagon, to compare with line-drawing dimensions, where available. To do this I use other items in the photographs for approximate scale if there is no scale drawing available. As well as the overall shape and size of the wagon, I also look at the layout of the lettering, numbers and any special notices and note similarities to other prototypes.

I look at the buffer type and pattern shown in service to see whether that differs from the official drawings, as well as the brake gear layout. Identifying the types of wheel used on the prototype is also important to replicate on your model; for example, the use of open or closed spoke wheels or three-hole disc wheels. Where bogies are present, I look at the type of bogie, the size of frames, the types of wheel and also the braking arrangements and location of brake levers.

All of this careful study and note-taking is carried out so that I can assess what components I am able to fabricate from raw materials, such as sheet brass, plasticard or wood, what parts I can modify from my stock of spares hoarded from the construction of previous kits and then determine what parts I might need to procure from a specialist supplier.

As part of my research, I use the internet to search for images of the prototype and to see if there is any reference to a kit in a different scale or gauge to that which I model. Looking at kits in other scales can be a useful guide to understanding how to put a scratch built model together to resemble the prototype and to show what level of detail might be attainable in model form.

I have a collection of books about the railway company and the period that I am particularly interested in from a modelling perspective. I have found that reviewing a wide range of books about the same railway company can provide all sorts of useful information about how the company was formed, developed and was run, and can also help to provide a 'feel' for the way that the company operated and how it used its rolling stock in its day to day operations.

Sources of data that I have found extremely useful and that can be used for a wide variety of railway prototypes include archive collections on-line; for example, The Great Western Archive (www.gwr.org) or The LMS Society (www.lmssociety.org.uk) provide modellers of these railway companies with an invaluable source of data. In addition, there are the more traditional physical collections held by museums and railway preservation societies that may be available for consultation.

There are also numerous factual text books that can be referenced on just about every main UK railway company, ranging from pre-Grouping, Grouping, Nationalization, Sectorization and subsequent Privatization, as well as most of the constituent companies that went to make up the big four at Grouping in 1923. The resource base is potentially huge and I would recommend that some consultation with these resources should form part of your research activities.

As part of the research and planning process for scratch building, I have also found that it is extremely useful to write out the potential construction steps that you plan to make for the construction of the model. At the same time, it is also prudent to think through the process of how the parts are going to join together, as this will determine your selection of materials for the project. There is no big secret process or skill here; if you have made plenty of model kits, you will have developed the knowledge and skills of understanding what will work in the scale you are modelling in and what will not work.

This process of planning how you are going to construct the model is particularly relevant when you are considering building either open wagons or vans. For example, when building a covered wagon or van, it means that you can be less concerned about what it looks like inside or too concerned about scale thicknesses for the sidewalls, as this detail will be hidden by a cover or roof. By contrast, with an open wagon, the interior detail is equally important as the exterior and one of the main considerations is that the sidewall thicknesses need to 'look right', as illustrated in Fig. 212.

Fig. 212 The wall thickness on open wagons is something that needs to look right when scratch building. To achieve scale wall thicknesses on this open wagon two layers of thin plasticard were laminated to provide strength.

The skills developed through building wagons and vans can also be applied to other rolling stock, such as coaches and locomotives. The process of carrying out research and thinking through the method of construction, as well as making notes on construction sequencing, are all relevant skills for building all sorts of subjects, not just rolling stock for your railway.

MAKING A START

Having carried out all of the research and decided on what you want to build, the next stage is to decide on whether you can achieve what you want from modifying a kit (kit bashing) or whether you wish to build from scratch. To some extent this will be governed by your willingness to accept compromises in the construction process or whether your goal is to achieve 100 per cent perfection and representation in exact scale of the prototype you are looking to reproduce.

Once you have decided that scratch building is the way forward, your first task should be to work through your notes and compile a list of components and materials that you will require to complete the project. It is better to carry out this process before

Fig. 213 The spare parts' box is an essential component of the modeller's tool bench, with a wide variety of small parts kept ready to hand.

Fig. 214 As well as hoarded parts from old kits and a supply of small components, items such as bogie kits and spare floor and roof sections also prove useful.

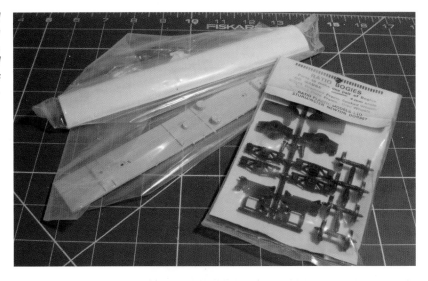

Fig. 215 To form van roofs when scratch building, the use of brass sheet provides a strong and sturdy roof, provides weight to a plastic model and all achieved at scale thicknesses.

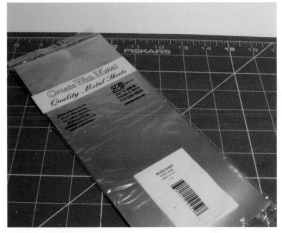

Fig. 216 A selection of specialist white metal parts, such as buffers, vacuum pipes, brake cylinders, brake levers and coupling hooks is useful to have in stock before starting any modelling project.

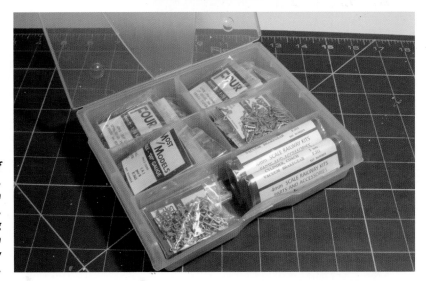

you start any building, as it can be extremely frustrating to get to a key stage in the build and then realize that you are missing a critical component.

To avoid this problem, I like to keep a stock of standard parts, such as the various common patterns of buffers, vacuum pipes, coupling hooks, vents, brake gear and brake levers, that I will likely need for the prototypes of the period and railway company that I model. I also keep a box of spare parts harvested from kits and a selection of useful materials such as plasticard in various thicknesses (most commonly 10thou, 15thou and 20thou), a selection of microstrip, plastic rod, fine wire and 10thou brass sheets. A stock of replacement wheels (I prefer to use Gibson OO fine-scale, but other makes are available), brass bearings and couplings are also extremely handy, as these can take time to arrive in the post if you have to order and you have no local model shop.

Once you have all the parts and components that you think you need, I have found it extremely useful at this stage to prepare a list of construction steps, similar to the instructions that you find with some kits, so that you can think through and write down how you are going to make something. This is the time when you can do trial dry runs of some of the key stages of assembly to check that what you think might work will actually work in practice.

I like to make some rough sketches as well, when I have tried the dry runs, to show key details; you may also find this a useful tool. These do not have to be high-quality pieces of artwork, as long as they mean something to you as the builder. As well as providing a useful *aide-mémoire* to the construction process, by writing the steps down, making a few sketches and adding to these notes as you work through the build, you will have an invaluable record of what methods and materials worked for future reference on other projects.

When you are sure that you have all the necessary parts and materials, and you have your notes on how you plan to make the model, then it is time to begin the construction process. I have found that the best place to start with wagon building is by forming the body and ensuring that this is square and level before adding the underframe. I then build the underframe to match the dimensions of the body. The sole bars and axle boxes can be added next and checked, using the wheel sets, to ensure that the axle alignment is perpendicular to the sides of the wagon and that the wheels run freely in the chassis.

Once the basic structure is completed, it is then time to move on to the addition of the detail components. With the construction of vans, I prefer to leave fixing the roof in place until the body work has been painted and decals applied accordingly. The fitting of fine detail parts and, in particular, fragile detail parts should be added as late as possible in the construction process to avoid the risk of damage from handling the model during construction.

With some subject types, it may be possible to break the construction of the wagon down to a series of sub-assemblies. This allows sections of the wagon to be built in isolation, including possibly some of the painting and fine detail work, before bringing the sub-assemblies together to complete the whole prototype. This sub-assembly approach is a good way of breaking down the work into manageable sections. These sections comprise work that can perhaps be achieved in one or two working sessions and avoids the risk or temptation to rush to complete something.

Using my first attempt at scratch building an OO gauge wagon as an example, having seen the type of wagon I wanted to build, the first task was to decide how to build a reasonable model in 4mm scale to represent this part of the everyday life of the railway. For the construction of my chosen subject, a Great Western Railway Cordon Gas Tank wagon, I started playing around unsuccessfully with various pieces of card and wood to try to obtain a satisfactory tank-like structure to the correct size.

The results were not particularly good and I subsequently identified, from browsing the internet, the 'N' gauge kits produced by PECO, specifically the kit for the 10T tank wagon (PECO ref: KNR-167). A quick comparison of the size of the tank in the kit with the dimensions of the tank type I wanted to build for the gas tank wagon, indicated a favourable fit and two kits were duly purchased. (A more detailed description of the creation of this model is provided in Chapter 7.) What this example shows is the need to have a clear understanding of what you are trying to build and to keep an open mind when looking for a source of materials for the scratch build project.

VISUALIZATION AND MOCK-UPS

One of the techniques that I make use of when making models from scratch, is to visualize what the final model will look like and, where necessary, to try out methods of construction using mock-ups. The idea is to get a good clear understanding in your mind as to what you are trying to achieve in model form before starting. This visualization process can be extremely useful and in the past I have made mock-ups of parts of a model that I am trying to build in order to see how it might go together and which material type would be the best for the task in hand. You may wish to consider this as a useful strategy for particularly complicated elements of a model, as the outcome of making a mistake with the mock-up is only some used card that can be recycled rather than using up more expensive brass sheet or plasticard.

In some instances it may also be possible to create a 'production line' for the fabrication of similar parts so that you can bring some degree of consistency to the production of parts and so that you do not have to spend time re-learning how you made something several times. Start by collecting together all the individual components (such as buffers, etc.) and materials (such as plasticard, brass sheet, etc.) that you will likely need, even to the point of considering different materials for each element to be built.

The whole process of making mock-ups allows you to assess whether your planned approach will work. It allows you to see whether it is possible to actually make something representative in model form and perhaps, most importantly, to determine whether it will be possible for the completed model to operate on your layout. This is where compromises in detail or accuracy may have to be considered in your model. For example, the ability of the finished model to negotiate the radius of curves on your layout and the coupling methods used for your rolling stock, to name but two, place constraints on the operation of the model that you will need to consider, unless the plan is to create a model that is just going to sit as a static display!

WALLS ON WAGONS

Forming the planking to represent wooden-bodied wagons and vans can be achieved in a number of ways. If you are considering plasticard as the basis for your scratch building, then you can consider using embossed plasticard, or form your own using plain plasticard. Various manufacturers produce plasticard that is embossed to represent wooden planking, which can be adapted to give a reasonable impression of the wagon body. However, the key issue

Fig. 217 Visualization and the creation of mock-ups when scratch building is a useful method to adopt to save wasting expensive materials. For the creation of a non-standard bogie, a card mock-up of the bogie frame and stretcher has been created before starting in brass section.

Fig. 218 To achieve scale wall thicknesses, laminated layers of plasticard provide strength to the open wagon. The outer plasticard overlays can be scribed with wagon planking and location of doors, corner plates and bracing strips marked from line-drawings.

with using this type of product is that the planking is generally all regular spacing and size, which if you compare to a typical railway wagon is not always the case.

An alternative approach would be to consider using a base layer of plain plasticard to form the basic shell of the wagon, on to which you can put overlays of either individual planks, or an overlay of the entire wall, with the planks scored onto the sheet to match the line-drawings of the wagon being modelled. The use of individual overlays for each plank would be a fiddly process and requires high levels of patience, but is likely to give the best effect. An overlay for the whole wall with scored planking to match the line-drawing would be quicker and less wearing on the patience and is the method I adopted for the construction of the GWR bogie open wagon described in more detail in Chapter 7 and shown in Fig. 218.

WAGON FITTINGS

After forming the basic structure of the wagon, the addition of detail wagon fittings brings the model to life as a representation in model form of the prototype. Detail components in brass, white metal and plastic are available from numerous suppliers for use by the scratch builder, or you can fabricate your own components from raw materials to meet the specific requirements of your project.

As an example of forming components from raw materials, the formation of door bolts, hinges and latches can be represented using scraps of plasticard, waste brass from frets, wire or white metal scraps recovered from cleaning the flash of cast components. All of these materials can be suitably shaped with a bit of imagination and careful crafting, and then fixed in place on your model.

The use of raw materials or pre-formed detail components depends on your requirements for the degree of accuracy and is the choice of the modeller. If the finished model is to be viewed from a distance of several metres on a layout, then the level of accuracy may be less important than if the model is for static display on your desk or museum display cabinet.

To form door hinges on the model of the GWR Mink F van described in detail in Chapter 7, I used oblong-shaped scrap pieces of plastic microstrip, carefully folded over the door edge, as shown in Fig. 219. To form the door bolts on the same model, I made use of fine wire recycled from Rioja wine bottles, suitably bent to shape and attached with cyanoacrylate.

Another example of a common wagon fitting is the presence of bonnet vents. Bonnet vents were used by many railway companies in the design of the end walls of vans to provide ventilation. These vents can easily be recreated in model form from either two small triangle shapes cut from 5thou plasticard for the ends and a flat section cut to size from the same thickness plasticard overlying the triangles, or a single piece of 40thou or 60thou plasticard cut to the correct overall size and then carefully sanded to a cheese-wedge shape, before fixing to the end wall of the van.

A further example of a common fitting is the use of angle iron bracing for the wagon walls, used on both vans and open wagons. To detail your model, these can be formed in one or two easy ways. One way is to take some appropriately sized pieces of microstrip and first form the horizontal section of angle iron on the wagon wall. Then take a second piece of the microstrip and fix to the first piece but at right angles, so that the microstrip extends

Fig. 219   On a van scratch build project plasticard microstrip has been used to form the doors, door hinges and bracing strips. Fine wire has been bent to shape to represent the door bolts.

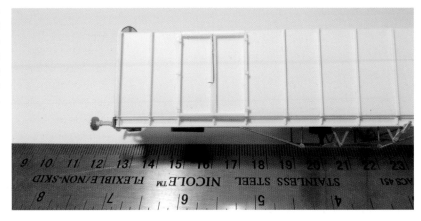

Fig. 220   On the end of the van, 'T' shaped plasticard microstrip has been used to form the bracing. The bonnet vent has been formed from a single piece of 40thou plasticard sanded to a wedge shape before fixing.

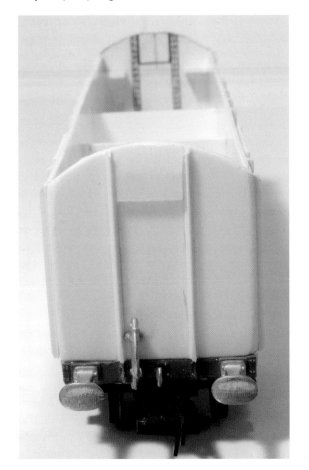

perpendicularly out from the wall of the wagon, as shown in Fig. 221. This can be a fiddly task, but with patience can produce excellent results, as shown in the example of the short cattle wagon conversion described in more detail in Chapter 5.

The second method of forming the angle iron bracing is to procure some of the fine detail extruded plastic 'L' section available from a number of suppliers. This is just cut to the correct length and fixed in place with minor fine adjustment with files or fine-grade sandpaper. I used this method with fine 'T' section extruded plastic section in the construction of the GWR Mink F bogie van described in more detail in Chapter 7 and shown in Fig. 222.

Fig. 221   A scratch built open wagon finished off with etched brass corner plates and plasticard microstrip used to form the angle iron bracing.

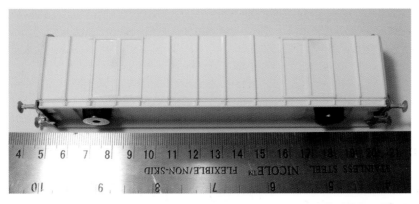

Fig. 222 Plasticard microstrip is available from a number of suppliers as flat strips, but also in many different shapes to aid the scratch builder. Extensive use of pre-formed 'T' section microstrip has been used on the van model to represent the angle iron of the prototype.

FITTING FRAGILE PARTS

When building wagons and vans the application of fine detail parts will, at some stage, mean that a true scale representation of these parts in 4mm scale will result in potentially extremely fragile components.

Making rolling stock that will be placed on a permanent layout and that will not get handled frequently, if at all, means the level of fine detail and representation of this as fragile parts is less of an issue. However, this does become a significant issue if you are making rolling stock for use on an exhibition layout or a temporary home layout, where there will be frequent handling of stock, transferring items from storage cassettes or boxes to layout and vice-versa.

It comes down to the practicalities of moving rolling stock and your acceptance of a compromise in the use of fragile parts in the final model driven by your planned end-use. This does not mean that rolling stock used on exhibition, or temporary layouts, should be devoid of detail – far from it, it is just a fact to be recognized that there is a greater risk of damage to the rolling stock when it is being regularly removed and placed on layouts or storage trays.

To reduce the risk of damage you can look to reduce the level of fragile parts by fabricating in such a way that the parts are supported by sections of the model, or by incorporating detail elements in with larger component parts and not as separate items. For example, where fragile parts, such as brake levers and tie rods, are included in your models, it might be sensible to consider only fitting them to the model at the end of the construction process and to fix them so that risk of damage is minimized. With Morton brake levers this could be accomplished by thickening the ratchet at the handle end so that it can be fixed to the axle box and the sole bar to reduce the potential for it to be knocked off or damaged through handling.

SCALE THICKNESES

In 4mm scale, 4mm represents 1ft in the real world! A statement of the obvious I know, but the number of times I have seen railway models with over-thickness parts, not just on rolling stock, but also in scenery and buildings, suggests that this is a common issue and likely to be a fault in the selection of the most appropriate material type for the job at hand.

Specifically, with respect to rolling stock, a typical plank width used on an open wagon was approximately 6 to 7in, but with some variance by railway companies and by use of wagon, between 4 and 9in. At 4mm scale, the plank size compromise would be to use 2mm for the average plank width on a wagon or van. For open wagons, the thickness of the planks, and thus the thickness of the sidewalls, varied, but typically the planks were between 2 and 4in, equating to between 1 to 2mm in 4mm scale (OO gauge).

To achieve realistic scale thicknesses and to build a wagon that is going to be reasonably robust for layout use needs careful consideration of material type and possible compromises on scale thicknesses. For example, during the construction of the GWR Tourn open wagon, I used 2mm as the average for plank width (on all four planks of the body sidewalls) and used 20thou plasticard to form the basic body shell, with 5thou plasticard for the overlays on which the plank detail had been scored by hand, as shown in Fig. 218. This combination gave a sidewall thickness of between 1 and 2mm. The model has proved to be robust and after a couple of years in use on my layout shows no sign of bowing of the sidewalls.

To provide some assistance, and as a point of reference on scale thicknesses, in Appendix 11 I have produced a table of the more commonly used dimensions scaled for modelling, including some common wheelbase and wagon body sizes.

MATERIAL CHOICE

It is important to consider how you choose the right material types for making components. The choice of material type has implications from a number of perspectives. The type of material can influence how components are made and can be fixed together, as not all materials can be used for the same component, as we have seen in Chapter 2 on the discussion of the relative merits and limitations of material types. The choice can also be driven by what the modeller feels comfortable working with, as well as what may already be available from the proverbial spares' box or workbench.

By way of an example, when making a model of a GWR Mink F bogie goods van, it was noted from the scale drawings and photographs of the prototype that the van body was made from iron and that the end walls curved in at least two directions, making the process of fabrication of this part of the body complicated. Furthermore, the drawings and photographs of the prototype showed that the roof profile was relatively thin.

To address these issues in model form, I chose to make the van body from 40thou and 60thou plasticard, as this material was easier to shape to get the curved corners to the end walls and at the same time match the roof arc as per the prototype, as well as

keeping the model quite stiff and strong. However, I formed the roof from 5thou brass sheet, suitably rolled to shape, as this is relatively thin and therefore more representative of the profile on the prototype, but this material provides a roof that is stronger than using plasticard at such a thin profile. (A more detailed description and accompanying photographs showing how this wagon was built are included in Chapter 7.)

TYPES OF ADHESIVES

There are numerous types of adhesive on the market to stick pretty much anything to anything. With the variety of material types available for use for model making, it is an essential part of the modeller's toolkit to have a number of different types on hand for use. Rather than describe all the types of adhesive that could potentially be used for kit and scratch building, not to mention the use of soldering for metal kits, I have decided to only include here some advice on the four main types of adhesive that I find most useful for my modelling requirements. I should point out here that I have no connection to the brands identified below, other than as a satisfied customer of the products used, and, of course, there are other products on the market that will do equally as good a job as the ones described below. As a note of caution, all of the adhesives listed here should be used in well-ventilated spaces, as the fumes, particularly from the first three examples described below, are not really good for your long-term health!

LIQUID POLYSTYRENE CEMENT

For the construction of extruded plastic kits and assembly of plasticard items I always make use of a liquid polystyrene cement. This type of adhesive works by breaking down or 'melting' the plastic of the two components where the liquid cement is applied and then, when the two parts are placed together and held in place for a few seconds, the parts bond together to form a strong joint.

For accuracy of placement of liquid cement I tend to favour the 'Revell Contacta Professional' product because of the approximately 25mm-long fine-needle

Fig. 223 *The use of a varied selection of material for scratch building necessitates the use of various specialist types of adhesive, such as impact adhesive, PVA, super glue (cyanoacrylate) and liquid polystyrene cement.*

applicator. The applicator allows only a small drop or thin stream of liquid cement to be discharged at once, giving excellent control over placement and volume of adhesive used. The long fine-needle applicator is also extremely handy for applying adhesive in difficult to access locations, particularly when applying additional adhesive on joints to strengthen them.

ALL-PURPOSE ADHESIVE

For other types of plastic that cannot be secured with liquid polystyrene cement, as well as for wood and metal components, I use 'UHU All-Purpose Adhesive'. This type of adhesive is available in squeezable tubes and is more of a gel than a liquid, which can be worked into areas of a model to reinforce joints. I find that this type of adhesive works particularly well where I need to fix components of different material types together and where I need to be able to gently adjust the parts before the adhesive sets hard.

CYANOACRYLATE ADHESIVE

This type of adhesive is available in liquid or gel form and I tend to use the 'Loctite Super Glue' brand in

liquid form for fixing all sorts of metal and plastic components together. As my soldering skills are not of the highest standard, I prefer to use this type of adhesive to fix brass kits together. The adhesive works extremely quickly and has to be handled carefully to prevent sticking your fingers together.

I have found that the best way to use this type of liquid adhesive is to have a small block of wood into which I have created a shallow hole with a 10mm diameter drill bit. This hole acts as a temporary reservoir for the adhesive and I apply the adhesive to the model using a thin piece of wire, which in my case is a straightened metal paper clip.

From experience, the adhesive works best if you apply a few small drops or thin smear of the adhesive to the parts to be fixed together, then press and hold together the parts for approximately 10sec. The parts should be securely held together after this time, but I then tend to reinforce the joint by using the wire to apply a small bead of the adhesive at the joint and allow the adhesive to be drawn into the joint by capillary action. The joints usually set within a few seconds, but left for twenty-four hours, the joint should form a strong bond.

POLY VINYL ACETATE ADHESIVE (PVA)

Whilst the use of PVA glue might not immediately spring to mind as a useful adhesive for rolling stock modelling, I use this type of glue for a number of tasks where the other adhesives discussed are not appropriate. The first use is for fixing together wooden components or parts for wagon loads. As wood is absorbent, I find that the use of PVA through a fine applicator nozzle on the glue bottle can be very effective for fixing wooden parts together or for fixing wood to plastic. The PVA takes up to twenty-four hours to fully harden off, so you also have time to make any adjustments to the parts before the adhesive sets.

The second use of PVA is for fixing glazing to brake vans, horse boxes, etc., because the adhesive dries clear and does not leave an opaque residue on the clear glazing sheet.

The third main use of PVA is related to the formation of wagon loads, tarpaulin sheets and their tie ropes formed from thread. For the formation of the coal loads described in Chapter 4, I used PVA to fix the load in place on the false floor and then dribbled diluted PVA/water mix through the 'coal' to hold the material in place – when dried it left a shiny sheen on some of the surfaces, reminiscent of real anthracite.

COMMON PROBLEMS

Unless you are extremely lucky, then on a first attempt at scratch building there is always going to be something that goes wrong, such as parts that will not go together properly, or as intended, or the choice of material does not allow you to create a satisfactory representation of the element of the wagon that you are trying to replicate in model form. Some of the more common problems and issues that arise have been tabulated with some comments provided on ways to mitigate the risk of occurrence.

This is part of the learning process; typically, errors or mistakes will occur during the construction sequence when perhaps not enough pre-commencement thinking has gone into the planned sequence of construction. Another common error is when, after construction is completed, you realize that detail parts cannot be easily painted, or they are completing inaccessible for later painting. This emphasizes the points made earlier about planning your work sequence, doing dry run assembly sequences and even considering the use of a sub-assembly construction process where practical.

Other problems typically occur around the selection and use of materials, as well as the fragility of components in the construction process. Given the likely desire to create a model that looks and 'feels right', there will inevitably be the need at some point to compromise on the level of detail or scale thicknesses in order to reduce the risk of damage to the model, either during construction or later during handling and use on your layout.

APPLICATION OF TECHNIQUES ELSEWHERE

The skills and techniques described in this book have equal application to other types of rolling stock, such as carriage building, which is only a big van with windows, and, to some degree, locomotive building. I have used the skills described here to scratch build four-wheel and bogie carriage stock, a fleet of wagons and vans, as well as locomotives for my OO9 narrow gauge that forms part of my layout.

As well as the use of these skills in expanding your fleet of rolling stock, the skills are also transferrable to the construction of buildings and structures for your layout. For example, I have scratch built a stone and steel girder road over a bridge on my OO gauge layout, using the same principles of research, drawing scale plans for the structure and planning a construction sequence. Another example of where I have scratch built includes the construction of a small Puffer coaster for a harbour scene on a colleague's extensive OO gauge layout. This ship was constructed as a waterline model, with open hold for loading and was almost entirely made from scrap pieces of plywood, timber, card and plasticard.

A SELECTION OF COMMON PROBLEMS

Problem	Comment
Access for painting detail parts	• Dry run assembly to check access • Consider painting parts prior to assembly
Fragility of parts	• Consider compromises on scale thicknesses • Consider choice of materials for fabrication • Fitting parts last where possible to reduce risk of damage
Parts do not fit together correctly	• Dry run assembly to check fit • Careful marking and cutting of materials, 'check twice, cut once' • Selection of material types and correct type of adhesive to join parts
Poor running qualities	• Misalignment of axle boxes, check with wheel sets when fixing prior to adhesive hardening • Use metal wheel sets and brass bearings • Consider use of rocking 'W' irons • Twisted bodywork (see below) • Lack of ballast or weight to the model (see below) • Check back to back of wheel sets
Twisted bodywork	• Set bodywork on flat glass surface during fixing, clamp, if necessary • Dry run assembly to check joints
Lack of weight to model	• Add ballast in side vans or under the floor of open wagons • Use of white metal and brass detail components to add weight to the wagon • Use of metal wheel sets and brass bearings
Too thick sidewalls	• Review scale thicknesses and selection of appropriate materials for components
Model does not look right	• Proportions incorrectly interpreted from scale drawings and photographs • Consider mock-ups to check dimensions and scale of components
Detail does not show after painting	• Too heavy paint application – consider alternative paint application techniques • Consider over-emphasizing detail to allow for painting

Fig. 224   Scratch building techniques described here for OO gauge have wider applications, an example of which is this selection of narrow gauge (OO9) coaches built from parts of old Ratio coach kits, card roofs and plasticard end walls.

CONCLUSIONS

The critical aspect of the scratch building process is patience. Do not rush, make sure you do dry runs, then critically review and do not be afraid to reject something, as you may regret that later. As those of a certain age will no doubt remember from their school days, 'measure twice and cut once' is a useful principle to adopt in your model construction and avoids frustration and the waste of materials.

Unless your model-making skills are exceptional, do not expect to make your first scratch build project without making mistakes or having to throw some element into the bin or recycling box.

CHAPTER SEVEN

SCRATCH BUILDING: WHAT CAN YOU ACHIEVE?

This chapter will cover a number of worked examples of the models that I have produced over the years to demonstrate what can be achieved, in the words of the *Railway Modeller*, 'by the average modeller'. I have chosen four models that I have scratch built to provide examples of a special wagon, a van, an open wagon and a flat wagon. The examples are all based on GWR prototypes, as that is the company and period that I model in OO gauge. Notwithstanding that, however, the observations and methods described in the following examples are generally applicable to a wide range of prototypes, scales and gauges.

SCRATCH BUILD 1: A CORDON GAS TANK WAGON

The first example included here for reference is the construction of a Cordon Gas Tank wagon, which was my first attempt at scratch building rolling stock. A short article based on this text was previously published in *Railway Modeller* (Tisdale 2010a), but a more detailed description of the scratch build process, with accompanying photographs, is provided here for the reader to understand the processes followed in the construction of this wagon.

BACKGROUND RESEARCH

The use of gas lighting in coaching stock led the Great Western Railway to construct a number of special tank wagons specifically to deliver oil and coal gas from the generating plant at Swindon Works to various stations around the GWR system, to allow local replenishment of gas to coaching stock reservoirs. Research shows that there was not one particular prototype example for these wagons, but rather that these wagons were built to various styles and sizes, typically utilizing underframes recycled from decommissioned old wagons and coaches.

At the time of writing the article, I was aware that there were a number of brass kits available in 4mm scale for the larger examples of vehicles of this type. However, at the time that I was considering making the model in 2009 I was not aware of a kit being available to represent one of the smaller examples, as illustrated in Russell (1971: figs 187 and 188). However, later research indicates that a similar prototype example was available as a white metal kit (produced by David Green) and I understand that more recently (in 2014) Falcon Brassworks has listed on their kit list an example of the smaller Cordon Gas Tank wagon.

Notwithstanding the availability of brass kits, I decided that I wanted to provide one of these smaller types of special wagon for my own OO gauge branch line layout, 'Llanfair', and settled on scratch building a representation of one of the smaller examples, as illustrated in Russell's book, specifically an example of the wagon that carried two longitudinally aligned gas tanks as shown in Fig. 225.

MATERIALS AND COMPONENTS

Having identified the type of wagon that I wanted to build, the first task was to decide how to build a reasonable model in 4mm scale to represent this part of the everyday life of the railway. This model was my first attempt into the sphere of scratch building, having previously only built kits from the various well-known manufacturers, such as Ian Kirk, Parkside Dundas, Keyser, Cambrian, Cooper Craft and Ratio; as well as a couple of the Shire Scenes brass side replacements for the Ratio four-wheel coaches and milk wagon, referred to as a Siphon C in the GWR telegraphic code.

I started by attempting to create a reasonable representation of the gas tanks, as these form the main focus of the model. After playing around unsuccessfully with various pieces of card and wood, attempting to obtain a satisfactory tank-like structure to the correct size and proportions, I was

Fig. 225 A scratch built GWR gas tank wagon to represent an unusual but essential prototype for a branch line railway.

Fig. 226 A collection of suitable parts from the spare-box and two PECO N gauge tank wagon kits to use as the basis for this project.

Fig. 227 The underframe assembly comprised suitable waste pieces of plastic card sheet for the floor. The centre-line of the floor and planks were marked on the plasticard with pencil.

not convinced that the end products were acceptable. So I turned to the internet for inspiration and identified, from browsing a number of sites, the N gauge kits produced by PECO, specifically the kit for the 10T tank wagon (PECO ref: KNR-167). A quick comparison of the size of the tank in the kit with the tank on the prototype I wanted to build indicated a favourable fit and two kits were duly purchased.

The rest of the parts for this scratch building project came from my spares' box and stock of specialist components. The buffer beams, sole bars, side frames and brake gear were derived from an old Ian Kirk van kit. Although these parts were not to the exact style and dimensions of the prototype, they were close enough – this was a compromise that I was prepared to accept on this first attempt at scratch building.

White metal upright vacuum pipes and standard pattern GWR wagon buffers (ABS or similar products) were used and OO gauge fine-scale 12mm diameter three-hole disc wheels and brass bearings (Gibson or similar) were selected for this model. In addition to these items, various pieces of plastic sheet, plastic rod, scrap white metal and wire were also collected together and used as detailed below.

CONSTRUCTION OF THE SUPERSTRUCTURE

Starting with the gas tanks, I took the N gauge tanks and tension bars from the PECO kits and stored the rest of the parts in my spares' box for future use (these items were subsequently used to form the basis for scratch built narrow gauge rolling stock for my layout, but that's another story). The tank bodies were then filled with scrap bits of white metal to provide ballast and then glued together with liquid polystyrene cement, as shown in the instructions for the kit.

Once set, the sides and ends of the tanks were sanded flush along the join line, using fine-grade sandpaper and needle files, taking care not to remove the rivet detail. The various fittings moulded on the upper part of the N gauge tanks were carefully removed with a sharp chisel blade craft knife, to produce a simple rounded-off tank body to match the profile of the prototype. I found that if the parts are carefully removed, the filler cap from the top can be re-used and, in my case, I re-affixed them to one end of each tank, as shown in the accompanying photographs, to represent filling points. The tanks were then put to one side whilst the basic wagon underframe was constructed.

Fig. 228   The modified tanks were positioned using the marked centre-line and counting the number of 'planks' from each end to ensure the tanks were evenly spaced.

Fig. 229   Steel ballast weights, brake gear and connecting rods were added to the underside to add detail.

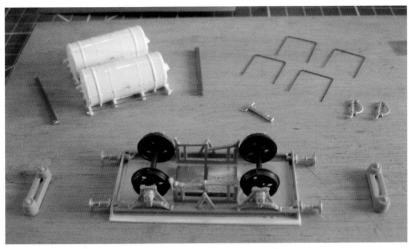

CONSTRUCTION OF THE UNDERFRAME

An underframe base was cut, approximately 59mm by 24mm, from scrap 2mm-thick plastic sheet. Mine was formed from waste Wills paving sheets, to which the wagon sole bars and side frames were glued, checking for vertical alignment and correct width for the preferred wheel sets. The width of the underframe base sheet will vary slightly, depending on whether you are using EM, P4 or OO gauge wheel sets. It is important to check the width of base required before you start cutting any materials. As has been noted previously, installing the brass bearings into the axle boxes on the side frames is easier to do before fixing the side frames to the underframe base.

The underframe assembly was put to one side and allowed to dry. In the meantime the wagon floor was prepared. I cut two sheets the same size (64mm by 33mm) from 0.5mm-thick plastic card to form a sub-floor and floor for the wagon. The sub-floor was glued to the underframe assembly, as shown in Fig. 228, along with the buffer beams.

The second sheet, which formed the visible floor of the wagon, was marked with a pencil at 2mm centres, measured from the wagon end, and lined parallel to the wagon end to represent the wooden planking of the floor (as shown in Fig. 228). The pencil lines were then scored with a sharp knife, but being careful not to cut through the sheet completely. The floor section was then glued on top of the sub-floor sheet and the model was then placed on a flat surface (glass tile) to allow the glue to harden off for at least twelve hours.

The buffer beams were then carefully drilled out to accept the ABS white metal buffers and an additional ballast weight (a Cooper Craft wagon weight) was glued to the underside of the under frame (as shown in Fig. 229). Once the ballast was fixed in place, the brake gear was installed, together with the connecting rods formed from 0.75mm diameter plastic rod. The wheels were installed to check free-running before the brake assemblies hardened off.

ASSEMBLY OF THE SUPERSTRUCTURE COMPONENT PARTS

The tanks were fixed to the wagon base with liquid polystyrene cement and checked to ensure that they were squarely aligned with the edges of the wagon floor and that the tanks were not twisted about their central axis, using the join lines in the tank-halves as a guide (see Fig. 230). To form the horizontal tension rods that sit on the outer side of each tank, pieces of 0.5mm wire were cut to length, sitting nicely within the preformed holes that are on the moulded end bar on the tank kit.

Fig. 230 With the tank positions finalized and the end beams in place at each end of the tanks, representation of the horizontal tension rods was added using the holes in the original kit for guidance.

Fig. 231 These types of wagons were considered part of the engineering stock and thus were painted black rather than the standard GWR wagon grey.

The 'U' shaped tension rods from the N gauge kit were then subsequently used as handrails on the access platform located at one end of the wagon (*see* Fig. 231). To install the handrails, I drilled 0.35mm diameter holes in the wagon floor ends to accommodate them, using a spot of cyanoacrylate glue to hold each piece of wire in place. Additional floor bracing beams were formed from scrap plastic sprues and added at each end of the tanks to match the layout indicated in the photographs of the wagon (Russell 1971) and as shown in Fig. 230.

The prototype included a hand-brake stanchion on the access platform at one end of the wagon. To rep-

resent this hand brake in model form without buying a bespoke part, I opted to form the stanchion from a piece of scrap white metal, suitably fixed to the wagon floor, as shown on the prototype in Russell (1971: fig. 188). I then took a piece of 0.5mm wire and bent it to shape to form the turning handle, before fixing the handle to the hand-brake stanchion (*see* Fig. 231).

I formed valves and feeder tubing from waste plastic and fine wire, respectively, with the wire recycled from the wire mesh commonly found on Rioja wine bottles. These were then added to represent the feeder points from each tank, as shown in Figs 231 and 232.

Fig. 232 *The fine handrails were formed from the N gauge kit tension rods. The hand-brake stanchion shown on the right-hand side of the model was formed from waste white metal.*

FINISHING TOUCHES

Once completed the whole wagon was then painted matt black as per the prototype described in Russell (1971), indicating that the vehicles formed part of the engineering wagon fleet of the railway company. HMRS Pressfix transfers were used to complete the model. Purists I am sure will spot details where compromises have been made, for which I apologize, but the intention was to provide a fair representation of an interesting prototype to run on my layout, rather than a 100 per cent accurate copy of the prototype in 4mm scale.

SCRATCH BUILD 2: A BOGIE GOODS VAN

The next worked example is the scratch building of a GWR Mink F bogie van using a variety of material types and making use of the specialist components aimed at the scratch builder available on the market today. This project is a re-working of a scratch building project idea originally described over thirty years ago in a short article in *Model Railway Constructor* (Lavey 1984), but using materials and components available today.

INSPIRATION TO BUILD A GWR MINK F VAN

Leafing through some old railway modelling magazines during a sort out of the library at my local model railway club (Jersey Model Railway Club), I came across a long-forgotten article by Mr K Lavey in the October 1984 edition of *Model Railway Constructor* about scratch building a Great Western Railway Mink F bogie goods wagon in 4mm scale. Lavey (1984) described how he went about this process, with the aid of a sketch of the floor of the model, a reproduction of the official line-drawings and a couple of photographs of the finished model. This set the seed of an idea for a new project to occupy my spare time during the long winter months.

A long time ago, back in the 1970s, when those Hovis adverts were all the rage on the television, you could actually buy a white metal kit of this particular prototype in 4mm scale, which I understand to have been produced by Hobbytime. Being only a child at the time, I obviously lacked the foresight to buy one of these kits and store it until I was old enough to appreciate it! If you are extremely lucky you might be able to pick up an unmade one of these kits on an

Fig. 233   These bogie goods vans had a 30T capacity and were built for mainline fitted freight services. The GWR bogie Mink F was an iron bodied van, but much larger than the more commonly known four-wheel version represented by the Ratio Models kit.

online internet auction site, but usually at a premium price.

Having re-read the article and then consulted my own reference books back at home, where I found copies of the official line-drawings and a number of additional photographs of the prototype in Russell (1971) and Atkins *et al.* (2013), I quite liked the idea of having one of these wagons to run on my layout. However, not wanting to take out a second mortgage to buy one of the old kits from the auction site, I subsequently decided to have a go at scratch building my own version of the wagon.

LIST OF MATERIALS REQUIRED

From my experience building this model, the following parts need to be sourced before starting the construction of the model:

- One pair of GWR plate bogies (Ratio Models ref: 126 or Cambrian Models ref: C73)
- One set of four white metal square shank/oval head buffers (ABS or similar)
- One pair of RCH white metal coupling hooks (ABS or similar)
- One pair of upright vacuum pipes (ABS white metal, or similar)
- Brass wire for underframe (1mm for queen posts and 0.5mm for trusses)
- Brass detailing kits for 'V' hangers, Dean Churchward (DC) brake levers and cranks (Mainly Trains kit MT236, or similar)
- Brass wire (0.45mm) for brake connecting rods
- Brass strip (3mm wide × 10thou) for additional 'angle iron' attachment to bogies
- Brass 5thou sheet for roof (KandS or similar)
- 40thou plasticard for floor and sides walls
- 60thou plasticard for end walls
- Buffer beams recycled from the spares' box or 60thou plasticard shaped as required
- 'T' section Plastruct (or similar) for body strapping detail
- 3mm 'U' section Plastruct (or similar) for the sole bars

- Choice of coupling – for my model I chose a pair of Bachmann mini-couplings, long type (Bachmann ref: 36-026)
- One pair of 8BA nuts, bolts and washers to affix bogies
- White metal weights to add ballast to the wagon
- Four axles with 12mm diameter three-hole disc wheels (Gibson) and brass bearings
- Fine wire recycled from Rioja wine bottle mesh to form door fixing bolts
- Assorted plasticard microstrip for building up door frames and door hinges
- GWR wagon grey paint for body and under-frame
- Matt white for van roof and brake lever handles
- Decals of choice – I used HMRS Pressfix decals

As we have reviewed in Chapter 2, there are a number of tools and adhesives that were required to construct the model. The following, in particular, were found to be most useful:

- Sharp craft knife (various blades)
- Liquid polystyrene cement
- Impact adhesive
- Cyanoacrylate (super glue)
- Needle files
- Archimedes' drill and selection of fine drill bits
- Fine-nose pliers
- Side cutters
- Tweezers
- Steel rule
- Set square
- Block of wood
- Glass tile
- A steady hand and patience!

WHERE TO START

The most obvious starting point initially had been to consider the idea of using the Ratio Iron Mink kit (Ratio ref: 5063) as a basis for conversion to a Mink F. However, as soon as the pieces of the Ratio kit were laid against the line-drawings for the Mink F it became apparent that the bogie goods' wagon was an altogether much larger vehicle, not just in length, but also the height of the wagon body, as correctly pointed out in the earlier article by Lavey (1984). This difference is also indicated in Fig. 234, which shows for comparison a finished scratch built Mink F van alongside a completed example of the Ratio kit, as described in Chapter 3. With this in mind, I therefore decided to build completely from scratch using a combination of plasticard and brass, with the exception of the wagon bogies, which were a modified Ratio product.

This approach to the scratch building of this wagon utilizes some of the comments noted from

Fig. 234   To give an indication of the significant size difference between the two iron bodied wagons, the four-wheel iron mink is shown on the left compared to the bogie van.

the work previously described by Lavey (1984), but I have suggested amendments and alternatives to the earlier method of construction and used different materials for some of the elements to produce my own model version of the GWR Mink F van.

CONSTRUCTING THE BOGIES

Starting with the bogies, I acquired a Ratio Plate Bogie kit and opted to replace the plastic wheels supplied with the kit with OO fine-scale Gibson three-hole disc wheels running in brass bearings. As with most of these types of kits, I drilled out the axle

Fig. 235 The Ratio Plate Bogie kit was modified with brass bearings and the addition of brass strips to the top of the plate frames to represent prototype strengtheners.

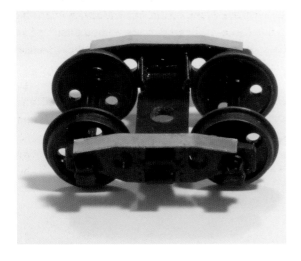

boxes using a 2mm bit and inserted brass bearings so that the shoulder was flush with the rear face of the axle box. Each bearing was held in place with a tiny spot of super glue applied to the bottom of the drilled out axle box prior to inserting the bearing.

To recreate the additional bracing applied to the plate wagon bogies used on the Mink F van, I took some 3mm-wide 10thou brass strip and cut to length (approximately 24mm long) a piece for each side frame of the two bogies (see Fig. 235). Then, using a pair of flat-jawed pliers on 'permanent loan' from my wife's jewellery-making toolbox, I gently bent the strip to match the top profile of the bogie side frame. When happy with the profile, I used super glue to fix the brass strip to the plastic side frames so that the strip was flush with the rear edge of the frame but overhung the front edge by about 1mm, as per the prototype example.

Incidentally, the flat-jawed pliers were supplied by Beadsmith, but other makes are available (see Fig. 25). These pliers are specially formed with flat jaw faces and 90-degree edges for jewellery making and as such I have found that they are also ideal for bending and shaping brass components for railway model making! The pair I have now 'acquired' appear to be very well-made and come at a reasonable price, at less than a tenner including postage.

In the Ratio kit the bogies are held on the bolster components by a push-in plastic plug. I wanted to be able to remove the bogies in the future for maintenance without the risk of splitting the plastic bolsters in the process, so I decided to use 8BA nuts and

Fig. 236 The standard bogie kit uses a push-in plug to fit the bogies to the wagon. For the construction of this scratch built wagon, the bogies were modified to accept 8BA nut and bolt fixings.

bolts, as this size of bolt can be just pushed through the preformed holes in the bolster and is a snug fit. To access the screw head of the bolt with a small screwdriver, a 3mm diameter hole was drilled in the centre of the bogie stretcher before putting the parts together. Once this had been completed, the bogies were then assembled as per the manufacturer's instructions, with the side frames fixed with liquid polystyrene cement to the stretcher (see Fig. 236). Before the cement had set hard, the wheel sets were installed to check free-running and that the frames were square.

The bolt was fed through a washer, the compensating pivot plate, to which the coupling was later fixed, and then into the bolster. The nut was screwed on and, when happy with the alignment, the bolt was glued to the inside of the bolster with impact adhesive. In addition, some scrap pieces of plasticard were also glued between the nut sides and the inside faces of the bolster to prevent it twisting off in the future.

The sub-assembly of bolt, washer and pivot plate was then inserted into the bogie side frames, as indicated in the instructions, by gently springing open the top of the side frames and dropping the pivot plate pegs into the guide holes on the internal faces of the side frames. On my layout I use tension lock couplings, so I used Bachmann mini-couplings (long type) fixed to the pivot plate in lieu of the ones supplied in the kit. The bogies were then ready for painting.

CONSTRUCTION OF THE WAGON BODY WALLS

I started with the walls of the wagon and measured out two pieces 140mm long by 27mm high on 40thou plasticard. Once cut out, I laid each sidewall on the line-drawing and using a soft pencil marked on the location of the vertical strapping and doors, as shown in Fig. 237. This makes the fixing of the strapping and building-up the door profiles easier than when the van body is completed.

The profile of the end walls of this wagon were curved in two directions: the curve around the top and the curved vertical corners to join with the sidewalls. This, on the face of it, makes it a difficult profile to replicate. However, taking the advice from the article by Lavey, I opted to use 60thou plasticard as he suggested for the end walls, with the sidewalls butting to the inside edge of the end walls.

To form the end walls I copied the line-drawings, cut them out and stuck them on to the 60thou plasticard sheet by flooding the paper with liquid polystyrene cement and leaving to dry. When dried, I cut out the walls around the line-drawing and then fixed one sidewall to one end wall, with the

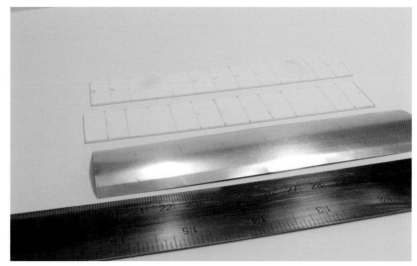

Fig. 237 The sidewalls were formed from 40thou plasticard sheet and each side was marked to show the location of 'T' bracing strips and doors. The roof, formed from 5thou brass sheet, was also marked with reference to the line-drawings to show the locations of the raised joints.

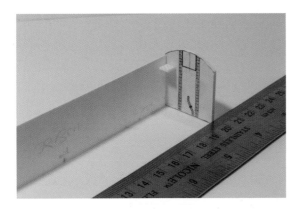

Fig. 238   To get the shape of the end wall, the line-drawing was photocopied, cut out and bonded to the end wall before cutting. Each sidewall and end wall sub-assembly was then constructed as a pair and checked to ensure a right-angle corner.

line-drawing on the inside face of the van and some scrap pieces of plasticard as bracing pieces in the corner towards the top of the sides (see Fig. 238). It is important to note here that the sidewall sits behind the edge of the end wall (see Fig. 239), the reason for which will become apparent when shaping the end wall to match the profile of the prototype.

The two sub-assemblies of one end wall and one sidewall were then glued together to form a box and placed on a glass tile to ensure that they were square. When the joints had hardened off, I then used files and fine glass paper to round off the vertical edges of the end walls to get the curved profile of the prototype. This is a slow process and calls for patience to make sure that the end profile looks correct, but when finished it does help recreate the feel of the vehicle prototype if you get the curved profile correct. On the model this has worked well, as once the ends were profiled and vertical strapping added, the join between the ends and sides was all but invisible (see Figs 240 and 241).

CONSTRUCTION OF THE WAGON BODY FLOOR

The floor of the wagon was cut out after the walls had been fixed together to form a box, so that I could measure the exact internal dimensions of the hole, as the floor sits within the box formed by the walls and flush with the bottom edge. The floor was formed from 40thou plasticard. The dimensions of the floor were measured from the internal faces of the body sides to give a rectangular section of approximately 140mm by 28.5mm; the exact measurement will depend on how well the body construction has gone together.

To accommodate the bolster fixing blocks from the Ratio bogie kit, the level of the bolster needs to coincide with the upper (inner) surface of the

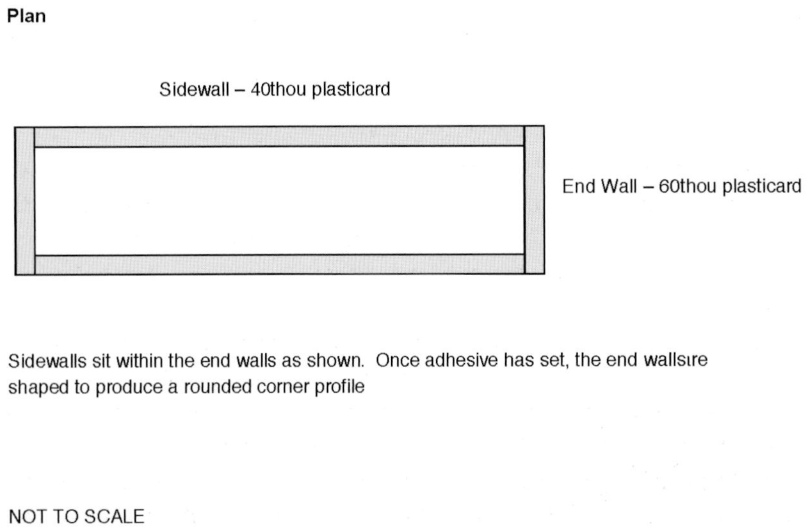

Plan

Sidewall – 40thou plasticard

End Wall – 60thou plasticard

Fig. 239   The sketch shows how the sidewall and end wall butt together at the joint, with the sidewalls fitting inside end walls. This was done to allow the shaping of the end walls as described in detail in the text.

Sidewalls sit within the end walls as shown. Once adhesive has set, the end wallsıre shaped to produce a rounded corner profile

NOT TO SCALE

Fig. 240 With the two sidewall/end wall sub-assemblies joined together, this completes the box forming the van body. The rounded off corners to the end walls are visible in this figure.

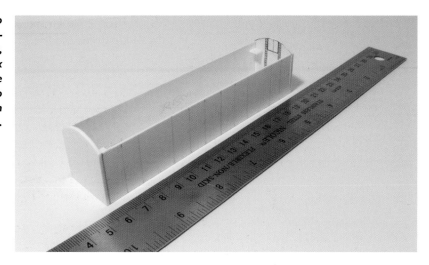

Fig. 241 The end-on view of the wagon shows the curved corners and the end wall marked for the later addition of bracing strips.

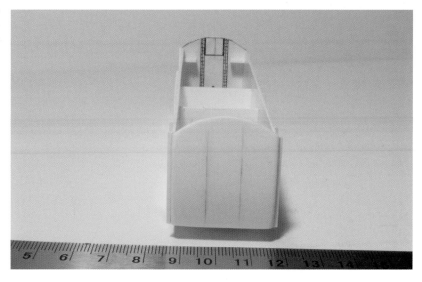

van floor. Therefore, I chose to cut the floor into three sections. The bogie centre-to-centre spacing measured from the scale drawing is approximately 100mm. Therefore, at each end of the van a section approximately 10mm was cut to fit immediately behind the buffer beam. A central section of floor, approximately 80mm in length, was cut and fixed centrally within the hole for the floor. To ensure it was central, the mid-point of the walls was measured and marked on the internal surface and similarly the floor section was also marked at its mid-point and the two marks lined up during fixing.

Additional pieces of plasticard were then cut to fix to the upper surface of the floors, creating a step in the floor at least 30mm long, as shown in Fig. 242. These steps allowed the bolsters to be fixed at the correct height for the bogies to sit below the sole bars (see Fig. 243).

At this stage it was important to consider how the bogies were to be fitted to the completed wagon. As described previously, I chose to fix the bogies with 8BA bolts so that they could be removed for maintenance and to allow separate painting as required. To accomplish this, the position of the bolsters was

Plan

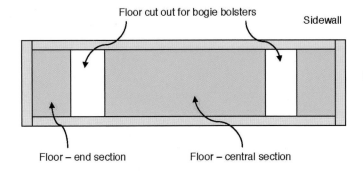

Floor cut out for bogie bolsters

Sidewall

End Wall

Floor – end section

Floor – central section

Section

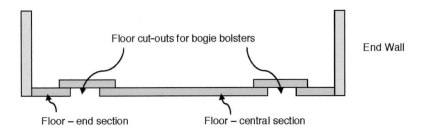

Floor cut-outs for bogie bolsters

End Wall

Floor – end section

Floor – central section

NOT TO SCALE

Fig. 242   To accommodate the bogie fixings and ensure that the wagon rode at the correct height, the floor was formed with cut-outs to accommodate bogie bolster fixing points, as shown in the sketch.

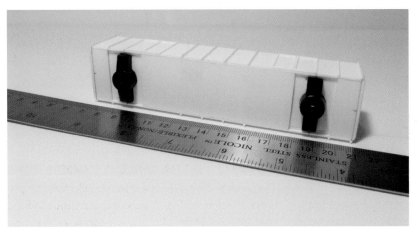

Fig. 243   Bogie bolsters fitted to cut-outs in floor of the completed wagon body. Before fixing these in place it is important to remember to glue the fixing nut inside the bolster first, as described in the text.

marked and a 5mm diameter hole was drilled in the raised sections of the floor so that the bolts could penetrate the floor. Alternatively, the bolts could be cut to length to avoid the need for the holes in the floor, but drilling a hole in the floor was deemed to be easier than cutting the bolts.

Ballast was then added to the wagon by gluing metal weights to the internal surface of the floor,

Fig. 244   Internal view of the van during construction showing the additional white metal ballast weight over the bogie fixing point to improve track adhesion.

Fig. 245   The completed wagon internal arrangement, including the internal bracing walls to reduce the risk of future bowing of the plasticard sidewalls.

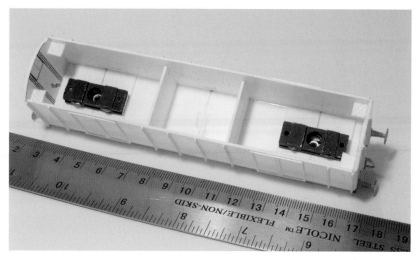

in particular around the location of the bogies to ensure the weights pushed the bogies down on to the track for good adhesion and running, as shown in Fig. 244.

Once the sections of floor had been fabricated and checked for fit, the parts were then inserted into the walls and checked to see that they sat flush with the bottom edge of the walls. To assist with this, the body was placed on a glass tile. When happy that the body was square and flush fitting, liquid polystyrene cement was fed along the internal joint between the walls and floor, and then the whole body was set aside to dry. Internal strengthening walls were

provided within the body to prevent later bowing of the van sides, as shown in Fig. 245.

DETAILING THE WAGON BODY

The prototype had prominent but relatively simple vertical strapping. To represent this on the model, I opted to use extruded plastic pre-formed 'T' section (Plastruct), available from model suppliers such as Hobby's. The vertical strapping was cut to fit each of the lines drawn on to the body sides, as described previously. The strapping was cut slightly over-long and then fixed with liquid cement, checking with a set square to ensure that each piece of strapping

Fig. 246   The prototype carried 'T' shaped angle iron bracing to the wagon walls. Pre-formed 'T' shape plastic strip available from Plastruct was used to form these bracing strips on the model.

Fig. 247   The pre-formed 'T' plastic strip was also added to the marked positions on the end walls. White metal vacuum pipes were also added at this stage.

was perpendicular to the base of the body. One side of the body was completed at a time and when the strapping had set, each section was trimmed to length with a sharp knife. The top edge of each strap was then filed to shape to match the profile of the end walls and to accommodate the overlap from the roof.

The vertical strapping on the end walls was added after the buffer beams were affixed, as the strapping extends over the joint between the wall and the buffer beam. Similar to the strapping added to the sidewalls, each part attached to the end was cut slightly over long and then glued in position. Once set, the strapping pieces were trimmed using a sharp

craft knife and then filed using fine files to match the profile of the end walls.

On the end walls of the prototype, simple bonnet vents were provided between the vertical strapping. To form these features on the model, I cut pieces of 40thou plastic card to size and then, using a careful slow process of sanding and filing, shaped the plasticard into wedge shapes. These wedges were then fixed to the end walls of the van and the top edge filed to match the curvature of the van body end walls, as shown in Fig. 248.

There were two double doors on each side of the wagon prototype and each double door had a heavy frame, with a profile depth matching the 'T'

Fig. 248   The bonnet vents on the end walls were formed from a piece of 40thou plasticard sanded to a wedge shape and then the top edge gently filed after fixing to match the profile of the end wall.

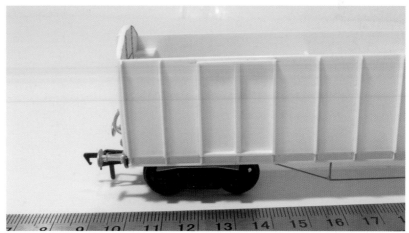

Fig. 249   The doors on the prototype were heavy duty. To reproduce this on the model, each door was built up from a number of layers of plastic microstrip cut to length.

strapping. To form this on the model, I chose to use micro-strip to the width of the door frame as marked on the walls, as described earlier. The door frames were built up with successive thicknesses of micro-strip to achieve the profile depth (see Fig. 249). I then used fine micro-strip scrap pieces for the door hinges and fine brass wire recycled from wine-bottle cages to form the door bolts. Once the detail parts had all set, the whole body was given a coat of spray paint (white) as an undercoat and regulating layer before applying the body colour.

CONSTRUCTION OF THE UNDERFRAME AND BRAKE GEAR

The sole bar was formed using 'U' section channel-extruded plastic strip, sized to match the size of the sole bar on the scale line-drawings. The channel was not fitted until the buffer beams had been fixed to each end of the body. The buffer beams were recy-cled from the spare parts' box and profiled using fine files to match the shape of the buffer beams on the prototype by checking against the line-drawings. Once the buffer beams had been fixed, the sole bar channel was cut to length by offering up the channel to the base and checking that it fitted flush with the back faces of the buffer beams. Pieces 2mm long of the same 'T' section Plastruct as used on the van body strapping were cut and fixed into the sole bar channel to represent the continuation of the body strapping to the base of the sole bar, as per the prototype.

The buffer beams were then drilled, as appropriate, to accept white metal RCH-type coupling hooks and GWR square shank, oval head buffers, which were fixed into the correct holes in the buffer beams using contact adhesive. Upright pattern white metal vacuum pipes were added to complete the end detailing.

On the basis of the photographic information and line-drawings that I have, the underframe on the prototype comprised a truss frame at each side between the bogies, immediately behind the sole bar. I formed the truss frames from brass wire, using 1mm diameter wire for the queen posts and 0.5m diameter wire for the connecting bars, as shown in Fig. 250.

The four queen posts were cut to about 10mm length and the location of the posts marked on the underside of the floor. Using a miniature Archimedes' drill and 1mm drill bit, holes were drilled in the floor for each post and then the posts glued into the holes with super glue, so that the posts extended about 6mm below the bottom edge of the sole bar.

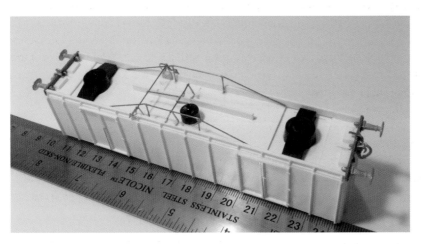

Fig. 250   To get the layout of underframe detailing correct it was marked on the floor of the wagon first. Each section of wire was cut and fixed in place to build up the underframe detail.

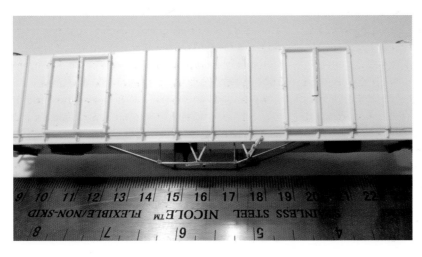

Fig. 251   A Mainly Trains etched brass detailing kit was used to supply the 'V' hangers and ratchet brake lever.

The connecting horizontal and diagonal bars were formed from individual pieces of 0.5mm brass wire cut to length after the queen posts had been fixed and stuck with super glue, starting with the horizontal bars in the middle and working outwards.

The DC brake handles, 'V' hangers and brackets were taken from Mainly Trains brass detailing frets for DC brake gear (Mainly Trains ref: MT236), with 0.45mm brass wire used to form the connecting rods. I found it easier to mark the layout of the 'V' hangers, connecting rods and brackets on the underside of the floor, using a pencil, before starting, so that I had a guide where each component needed to be fixed. I also found it easier to make up the DC brake handles, as well as bend and shape all the other components, before starting assembly, as this seemed to make the construction process easier to complete.

The vacuum brake cylinder was located on the underside of the floor first, off-set from the centreline as per the prototype. I then added a further piece of U-section Plastruct, the same dimension as that used for the sole bars, to provide a central beam under the middle of the floor, parallel with the sole bars. From this the various 'V' hangers and connecting rods could be constructed to provide a representation of the brake gear for the wagon.

FORMING THE WAGON ROOF

The roof profile on the prototype was relatively fine and was curved to match the end walls, as well as having each corner rounded off. As the body of the model wagon had been constructed predominantly of plasticard, I decided to use sheet brass for the roof. I used KandS 5thou brass sheet, cut 145mm by 36.5mm and then curved to match the end wall profile. The sheet was curved by rolling it gently around a cardboard tube from the centre of a roll of kitchen foil. For best results, the formation of the roof has to be done carefully, a bit at a time, with the rolling repeated until the correct profile is achieved. This process of forming the correct roof profile requires patience, but when completed the overall effect is worth the effort. When finished, the roof was given an undercoat of spray paint.

Even though the roof profile had been formed by rolling, the brass sheet retains some springiness and the curvature of the roof when rolled was slightly larger than the curve of the end wall profile. This was done so that the roof would want to spring up in the centre and reduces the risk that over time it might sag. The roof was fixed to the walls with impact adhesive, after the body had been painted, and was held in place with elastic bands for a period of at least twenty-four hours for the impact adhesive to set hard.

The corners of the roof were rounded off to match the shape of the prototype, using a pair of sharp scissors and fine files to form the basic shape before finishing off with fine glass paper. The strapping detail on the roof was formed using fine microstrip. The microstrip was cut over-long and fixed with contact adhesive. Once set, the strips were trimmed with a sharp craft knife and then the whole roof was painted white.

FINISHING TOUCHES

The body, underframe and bogies of the van were painted all over GWR wagon grey, whilst the roof was painted white, along with the DC brake handles. When dry, HRMS Pressfix transfers were used, using the photographs of the prototypes for guidance on positioning and sizes.

SCRATCH BUILD 3: BUILDING AN OPEN WAGON

The third example of scratch building is the construction of a GWR Tourn wagon. The text is based on an article published in the *Railway Modeller* in August 2014 but provides a more detailed description.

As is well known, the GWR had a whole list of weird and wonderful names, or telegraph codes to be accurate, for the wagons and vans used on their system. The first question from non-GWR devotees would probably be, so what was a 'Tourn'? Well it is my understanding that the word 'tourn' means either spinning wheel or, in medieval English, refers to the circuit or 'tour' that a Sheriff would undertake to administer law and order in the Shires. All

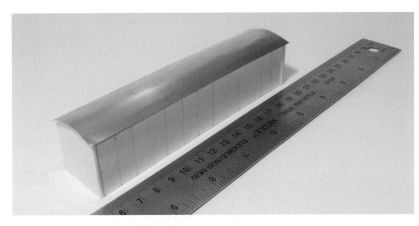

Fig. 252   The roof for the model was formed from rolled 5thou brass sheet, using the cardboard inner tube from a roll of tin foil as the forming tool.

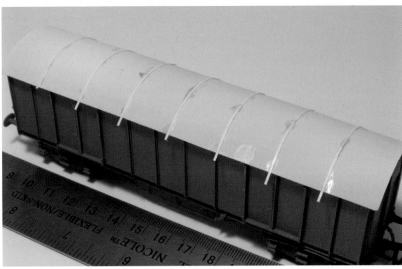

Fig. 253   After priming the roof and checking the marked positions for the raised strips, microstrip was used to add the detail. Each strip was cut over-long and fixed in place, then trimmed flush once dry.

Fig. 254   The painting is standard GWR wagon livery, with the details of the decals taken from reference photographs of the prototype.

Fig. 255   A one-off bogie open wagon constructed by the GWR presented an unusual prototype to model.

interesting stuff but I am not sure what the connection is between these definitions and a piece of
railway rolling stock dating from around the end of
the nineteenth century. Putting the history lesson to
one side, let us now explore how this scratch build
project developed.

INSPIRATION TO BUILD A TOURN

I stumbled across a line-drawing of this particular
bogie open wagon whilst browsing through my copy
of Russell (1971), looking for something else, and
was intrigued by the unusual nature of the wagon, as
it differed from the standard GWR rolling stock. On
this basis I decided to try and recreate the wagon
in model form for running on my layout. Having
decided to create a model, I then set about search-
ing through my collection of un-built kits, hoarded
spare parts and pieces looking for inspiration. I came
across parts from an old Ratio Bogie Bolster 'A' kit
(Ratio kit ref: 5062), from which I had used several
bits on other things, but which still had the floor sections, sole bars and bolsters to which the bogies are
fixed. This provided a basis from which to begin the
model and the ideas developed from there.

In terms of this specific piece of GWR rolling
stock, and based on my limited knowledge of the
subject, it is my understanding that this wagon was
a one-off bogie open wagon, intended by the GWR
as an experiment and built around the end of the
nineteenth century. The line-drawing (Russell 1971)
that I used for reference indicated that wagon was
36ft long over the headstocks, with an internal clear
loading area of 35ft 7in shown on the line diagram.

The notes with the line-drawing indicated that the
wagon was rated to carry a load of up to 25 tons and
ran on two short-wheelbase (4ft 10in) four-wheel
bogies. Other than being an experiment I am not
sure if there was a specific purpose for building the
wagon, but I would be happy to know more if anyone
has any further information.

Russell (1971) has reproduced a line-drawing of
this wagon in appendix 2 of his book, but unfortunately no photograph was included. I have searched
through the texts that I had in my small collection
of railway texts at home at the time of building this
model, but I could not find a photograph in any of
them of this prototype and I was unable to locate
one following a search on the internet. The absence

of a photograph of the prototype made the job of constructing the model a little more challenging and required some lateral thinking to look at the way other wagon prototypes from this period were put together and to use this information as guidance as to how this wagon might have been built.

This scratch building project was, therefore, my interpretation of what this wagon might have looked like, using only the line-drawing for guidance. I built the model to OO gauge, 4mm scale and although not a 100 per cent accurate reproduction, I believe that it is a fair representation of an unusual prototype.

LIST OF MATERIALS REQUIRED

The model was built using a variety of materials, but principally plasticard and brass strip and the lefto-ver bits and pieces from an old plastic kit. To assist the reader, should you wish to have a go at this project yourself, I have compiled the following list of materials that were used in this scratch build project and which you will need to collect together before starting:

● Selection of plasticard sheet (10thou and 20thou) and microstrip (Slaters)

Fig. 256 Parts for the sole bars and axle boxes were recycled from the spares' box.

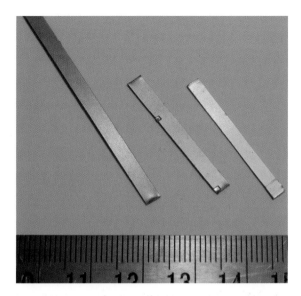

Fig. 257 Proof of the maxim that 'it will always come in handy' – a number of pieces of recycled brass strip waste from previous brass kits could be used for the bogies.

● Selection of brass strip (10thou) recycled from previous brass kits, as well as new pieces
● Etched brass wagon detailing kits, brake gear, corner plates, strapping, etc. (Mainly Trains)
● GWR Bogie Bolster 'A' – floor sections, sole bars and bogie bolsters (from Ratio kit ref: 5062)
● White metal GWR unfitted wagon buffers (ABS or similar)
● White metal coupling hooks (ABS or similar)
● 12mm diameter metal eight-spoke wagon wheels and brass bearings (e.g. Gibson/ Romford)
● Steel wagon weights left over from wagon kits to add ballast
● 10BA (or similar) nuts and bolts to attach bogies

BOGIE CONSTRUCTION

I started with the construction of the wagon bogies. Having studied the line-drawing of the Tourn and lots of photographs of other GWR bogie goods' wagons, it was apparent that the pattern of bogie used on the Tourn was not a standard GWR goods' wagon bogie, such as a plate or diamond frame. For some wagons, the GWR used converted old coach underframes and bogies, such as the Bocar wagons, but again the photographs and drawings that I have of these various types did not appear to match the size or pattern of the bogies shown on the line-drawing for the Tourn.

Therefore, without a standard design to copy from a photograph, I decided to scratch build the bogies using brass strip to match the line-drawing. Scaled from the line-drawing, each bogie frame for the model was approximately 39mm long by 24mm wide, with a frame height of about 3mm. Initially, I built a mock-up of the bogie frame sides and stretcher using thin card to get an idea of the dimensions (see Fig. 258) and to work out the best sequence for construction.

Once happy with the general arrangement and sequence of build, I then used a selection of 10thou brass strip recycled from previous etched brass kits, as well as pieces of strip, to form the frame components (see Fig. 259). Each of the long sides

Fig. 259 The first attempt at a scratch built bogie with brass strip and a brass plate for the bogie stretcher.

I cut to exactly 39mm. The end pieces I cut to a length of approximately 28mm to allow a fold back tab at each end, on to which I could affix the sides. I then built up the frames one side and one end piece at a time, ensuring that I got a 90-degree corner at each joint. When completed I then joined each sub-assembly together to get the completed rectangular frame for the bogie.

A 10mm-wide section of 10thou brass strip was then cut to form the stretcher, with fold-up tabs at each end. I first tacked this in place with super glue, with the stretcher surface flush with the top edge of the frame (see Fig. 259), but found that this presented the bogie with too much 'air' between the bottom of the sole bars and the top of the bogie frame. I therefore separated the stretcher from the frame, inverted it so that the face was flush with the bottom edge of the frames (see Figs 260 and 261) and this proved to be much more acceptable. At the same time, I marked the stretcher with the wheel locations and filed a notch in each location to ensure that it cleared the flanges. A hole was then drilled in the centre of the stretcher to accommodate the fixing nut for the bogie. This whole process was repeated for the second bogie.

Fig. 258 As the bogie used on the wagon appeared to be a non-standard type, a card mock-up of bogie frame and stretcher was built first to see what it would look like.

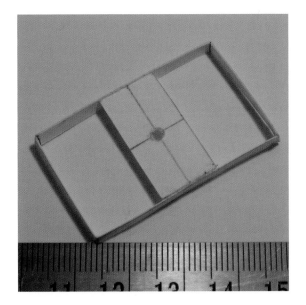

Fig. 260 Test-fitting of the prototype bogie revealed that the stretcher was too high. This is the second attempt at the bogie with a lower stretcher, including bolster with fixing bolt.

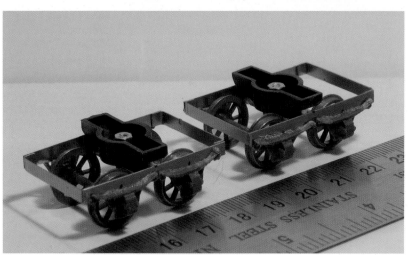

Fig. 261 The final version of the scratch built bogie with bolsters in place to fix to the floor of the wagon.

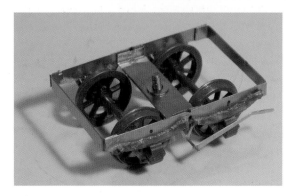

Fig. 262 The brake lever detail fabricated from etched brass parts and temporarily fixed to the bogie. These parts are very fragile and best left to the end before fitting to prevent damage during construction.

On the prototype, the axle boxes were at 4ft 10in centres, which equates to approximately 19mm in 4mm scale. To locate the axle boxes accurately on the model, I first marked the centre point of the bogie side frame and then measured out from this the centre-line for each axle box centre-line. The axle boxes that I used on the model were plastic parts from my spares' box, derived from previous kits. I modified these to match the pattern on the line-drawing by first cutting away the section that would be used to fit to the back of the sole bar. Then I carefully cut the joint between the 'W' iron and the spring, and bent the spring upwards while pushing the 'W' iron bits inwards at the same time, as shown on the photographs. I then inserted brass

Fig. 263   Bogies completed and track tested to ensure smooth running prior to fixing to the wagon. It was necessary to file 'V' notches in the stretcher plates to ensure the wheel flanges did not catch.

Fig. 264   The wagon body was built in two sidewall and end wall sub-assemblies to ensure right-angle corners. When set, the sub-assemblies were fixed together.

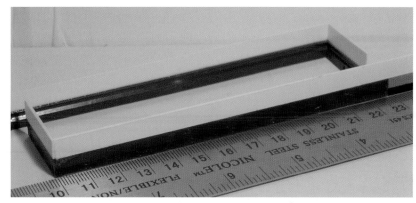

bearings and glued them to the bogie frames using the centre-line markings. At this stage, I inserted the wheel sets to ensure that the axles were square and free-running.

I assumed that the arrangement for the brake shoes and brake lever was common for both bogies in the construction of this model. Brake shoes were fitted to one side of each bogie, as indicated on the line-drawing, with a lever fitted to the bogie. I used plastic brake shoes cut from spare wagon brake gear assemblies and fixed them directly to the underside of the stretcher and in line with the wheels. The 'V' hanger and short brake lever came from a Mainly Trains etched brass wagon brake gear fret. The 'V' was modified to fit the bogie and fixed to the underside of the stretcher. A short piece of fine wire was then glued into the connecting rod hole at the base

of the 'V' to extend far enough out from the side of the bogie, so that the lever, when fixed to the other end of the wire, would stand proud of the axle boxes.

Fitting of the brake gear and lever I found to be quite fiddly and needed plenty of patience to get it square (see Fig. 262). From my experience, it would be advisable to leave attaching the brake gear and brake handle to each bogie until later, as these are quite fragile parts and it would avoid the risk of damaging this fine detail during the construction of the rest of the wagon and testing.

BODY CONSTRUCTION

Moving on to the construction of the body, I took the sole bar sections from the Ratio kit and removed unwanted moulded detail. I then extended the length

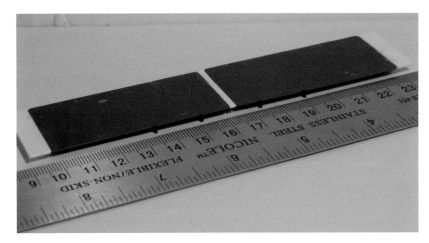

Fig. 265 The wagon floor was formed from pieces of an old bogie flat wagon floor sections from the spares' box and pieces of plasticard sheet of the same thickness (shown as white in the figure).

of each of the sole bars by 15mm at one end, using left-over sole bar sections from another kit. One could use brass section or plasticard to form the sole bar from scratch, but I opted to modify what I already had available. The sides and ends of the wagon body were then built up using 30thou plasticard to the full height of 11mm above the sole bar/ buffer beam, as shown in Fig. 264. I then joined one end and one side together, checking to ensure a square joint, and left them to harden off.

The next job was to construct a floor section, which needed to be 144mm long to fit within the body sides. I started with the floor section from the Ratio kit, which was in two halves and with a combined length of 128mm. I removed the moulded pips for the timber bolsters on the upper surface and scribed the floor with planking to match. Using 40thou plasticard, I added a 2mm-wide section between the two halves and a 7mm-wide section at each end to get the correct length (see Fig. 265).

The plasticard was scribed with planking to match the rest of the floor and when the glued sections had hardened off, I shaped the edge profile of the new sections to match the original kit parts. The reason for adding the sections was to retain the bogie locating points on the underside at the correct distance from the buffer beams, to match the prototype, and to ensure that these points were spaced equidistant about the centre-line of the wagon, as shown in Fig. 265.

Once the two side section sub-assemblies had hardened off they were glued together and placed on a glass surface to check that the body was square. The floor was then dropped in from the top and glued in position. Depending on your cutting work to date, this is the opportunity to fill any small gaps between the floor and sidewalls – I know that's what I had to do!

Fig. 266 Overlays for the wagon body were produced using 10thou plasticard. The overlays were scored to represent the wood planking on the wagon.

Fig. 267   Sidewall and end wall overlays were scored and the locations of the doors and strapping detail marked by reference to the line-drawings.

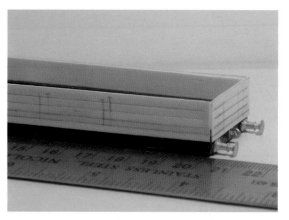

Fig. 269   The overlays were fixed in place with liquid polystyrene cement, starting with one sidewall and then working in one direction around the wagon, checking that the planks aligned at the joint.

This was the basic body shell completed; now it was time to produce the overlays for each side with the detail scribed on to them. For the overlays I used 10thou plasticard cut to 144mm by 11mm for each of the sides and 31mm by 11mm for each of the ends. As the 10thou plasticard is quite thin, I was able to lay the pieces over the relevant part of the line-drawing and, using a 0.5mm drawing pencil, trace the planking on each piece. I then scored along the pencil lines with a small, old electrician's screwdriver (see

Fig. 268   Each overlay was lined up against the body to check the fit. The plank detail was not continued to the end of the overlay as this area would be covered by the etched corner plates on the finished model.

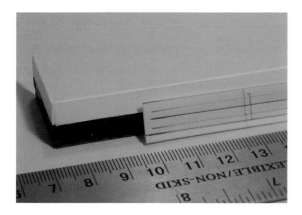

Figs 266, 267 and 268) to provide a representation of the plank and floor detail. The overlay sections were then fixed to the sides of the body shell using liquid polystyrene cement (see Figs 269 and 270).

The next step was to add white metal GWR wagon buffers and scale coupling hooks to the buffer beams. To fit the buffers, the surface plate detail on the buffer beams was removed with a fine file and the locating holes reamed out with a 2mm diameter drill bit prior to inserting the buffers and fixing with a spot of contact adhesive. The holes for the white metal coupling hooks were opened out with the tip of a craft knife and the hook fitted and glued in the same way as the buffers (see Figs 269 and 270).

The line-drawing showed that there were two drop-down doors, each 5ft wide, on each side of the wagon, spaced equally from each end of the wagon. To represent these on the model, the positions of the two doors were measured and marked on each side; specifically the positions of the vertical strapping and door hinges for each door (see Fig. 271).

Using a brass wagon detailing kit (Mainly Trains ref: MT164) the length of strapping was measured, cut and fixed, as appropriate, to represent the vertical strapping and hinge details for the doors (see Figs 272 and 273). The riveted brass corner plates

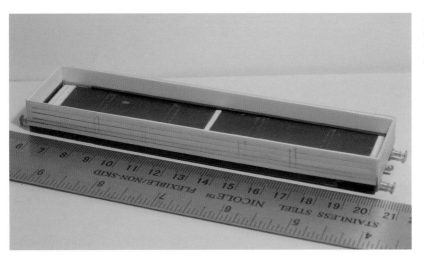

Fig. 270 With the bodywork completed, the next stage was to add the etched brass detail parts.

Fig. 271 A view of the underside of the wagon body showing bogie fixing lugs. These were positioned to ensure that the bogies were correctly located under the wagon to match the line-drawings.

Fig. 272 Etched brass rivet strip was used for the bracing and door details and corner plates added to hide the join in the overlays.

Fig. 273 A close-up of the rivet strip detail around each door location, including the representation of the door hinge with tiny pieces of brass rivet strip shaped to fit.

for the body were then cut to size from the detailing kit, folded to match the body, then fixed to the body with super glue, as shown in Figs 272 and 273. In addition, brass rivet strip was also cut and fixed to the end walls to match the line-drawing and then microstrip plasticard used to form the angle iron to the riveted strip, as shown in Fig. 274. To provide some additional ballast to the model, wagon weights, unused from previous models, were fixed to the underside of the wagon, as shown in Fig. 275.

At this stage it was time to fix the bogies to the body shell, to check the height of the bogies and, where necessary, provide packing to get the correct position relative to the sole bar. Once happy with the clearance between sole bar and bogies and the general appearance of the wagon when placed on

Fig. 274 On each end wall the bracing details required the use of brass rivet strip and plastic microstrip to get a good representation of the angle iron detail.

Fig. 275 With the bogie bolster fixed in place, additional steel ballast weights were added around the bogie locations to improve track adhesion of the finished model.

Fig. 276 A test fit of the bogie, with close up detail showing the single side brake shoes formed from bits of wagon brake gear cut and bent to shape.

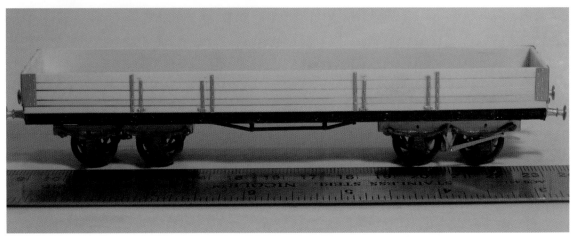

Fig. 277 The addition of truss rods formed from more pieces salvaged from the spares' box completed the scratch built wagon, apart from painting.

a section of track, the plastic bogie bolsters were fixed to the underside, having first fixed the holding nut for the bolt to the inside of each bolster using cyanoacrylate adhesive. The bogies were then fixed to bolsters with bolts, using a metal washer as a spacer between brass stretcher and plastic bolster, as shown in Figs 276 and 277.

The final part of the detail to be added was to form wagon trusses for the underside of the body (see Fig. 277). This could be done using brass wire or plastic rod, as appropriate. However, for this model I found that if the inner truss rods from the Ratio

kit were carefully cut down and shaped they proved to be the perfect size and proportions. Once modified these pieces were fixed to the underside of the body immediately behind the sole bar using liquid polystyrene cement.

FINISHING TOUCHES

The model was painted all over in GWR freight wagon grey, with the ends of the brake levers picked out in white. HMRS Pressfix transfers were used to complete the model, as shown in Fig. 278. The layout of the decals was pure guesswork on my

Fig. 278 The layout of the decals is the author's interpretation based on other wagon prototypes. No photograph of the completed prototype was identified at the time of construction of the model. Since completing the model, however, additional information suggests that the location of some of the decals is not quite accurate. The wagon has not yet been back to the wagon repair shops to be updated.

part, as I have no picture of the prototype to follow. However, I have based my assumptions of the location of each decal from studying numerous pictures of other GWR wagons to get a feel for how the lettering might have been positioned.

I am satisfied with the finished model and its general appearance; however, since preparing this work, I have found a picture of the prototype in Atkins *et al.* (2013) and my interpretation of what the bogies looked like was not too unreasonable, although the layout of the decals on my model was less accurate.

SCRATCH BUILD 4: CREATING AN OPEN CARRIAGE FLAT WAGON

The question as to what to do with the parts left over from the small MEX conversion of the Cooper Craft W1/W5 cattle wagon kit (described in Chapter 5) was the inspiration behind this scratch building project. I was considering what to do with them, whilst browsing through my copy of Russell (1971) when I came across the Serpent family of vehicles with an 11ft wheelbase, specifically the vacuum fitted Serpent C (post-1943 referred to as CARFIT). This looked like a useful addition to my fleet of wagons, so I set about checking dimensions and identifying what spare pieces I had to hand.

LIST OF MATERIALS REQUIRED

The parts required for this project included the floor, sole bars, break gear and vacuum cylinder left over from the cattle wagon kit. However, for those wishing to reproduce this model but do not have these parts lying around, an alternative source would be the Cooper Craft 11ft wheelbase underframe kit (Cooper Craft ref: 1013). In addition, the following items were sourced before commencing work on the project:

- GWR pre-group 20in buffers (ABS white metal or similar)
- GWR wagon hanging vacuum pipes (ABS white metal, or similar)
- Alan Gibson eight-spoke wagon wheels and brass bearings
- Buffer beams and coupling hooks from spares' box
- Selection of plain plasticard, plastic microstrip (flat and square section) and plastic rod
- Two standard matchsticks (with heads removed)
- Approximately 4in or 100mm of fine chain
- Couplings of preference
- Paint and transfers

Fig. 279 *A simple open flat wagon produced by the GWR and referred to as an open carriage truck, shown with a covered car load.*

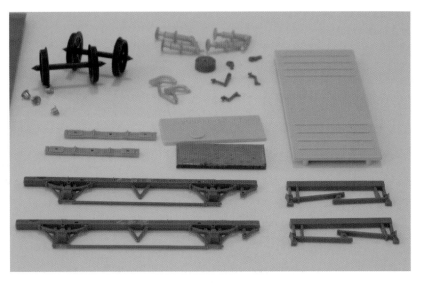

Fig. 280 *After completing the conversion of the cattle wagons described in Chapter 5, there were a number of parts left over.*

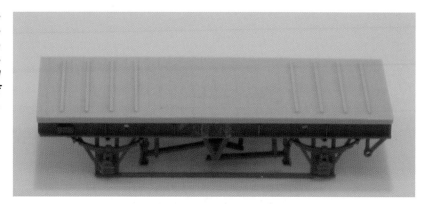

Fig. 281 The underframe and wagon floor were constructed and the wagon floor modified with the removal of the longitudinal ridges from the middle of the floor.

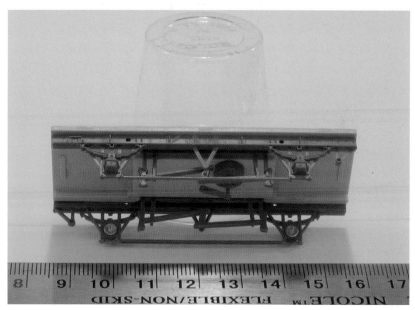

Fig. 282 Brass bearings were added for the replacement wheels and brake gear fixed in place ensuring alignment with the wheels.

CONSTRUCTION OF UNDERFRAME

Starting with the floor of the cattle wagon, the first action was to remove the longitudinal raised strips in the middle of the floor section, using sandpaper/fine file, and then to re-scribe the floor planking. I chose to retain the raised strips at each end of the floor that are parallel with the planking, but if preferred these can also be removed.

The next step was to take the sole bars and remove the two raised vertical mouldings (above the 'V' hanger) in the centre of each bar that are used to support the door stops on the cattle wagon kit, as these were not required on this wagon. Then the axle boxes were drilled out as required with a

2mm diameter bit to ensure a flush fit of the brass bearings. Once happy with the sole bars, these were glued to the floor section and the wheel sets installed to check that they ran freely and that the sole bars were square and vertical.

The ballast weight was glued into the recess on the underside of the floor (as per the kit instructions) and then the vacuum cylinder and brake gear added, again checking with the wheels to ensure free-running. The brake rod connections between the vacuum cylinder and the brake gear were then formed from plastic rod. I chose not to reproduce the rod connections to the brake lever at each end of the wagon as my choice of tension lock coupling

Fig. 283   The buffer beams were fabricated from spare parts with white metal buffers.

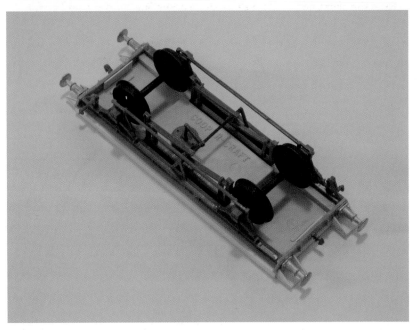

Fig. 284   Underframe detail comprised a vacuum cylinder and connecting rods. One of the unique features of this type of wagon was buffer cover plates for vehicle loading. On the model these were fabricated from plasticard.

and mounting block would not leave sufficient space to accommodate the rods. If you choose to use three-link couplings, then the rods could be added. The whole underframe was then left to harden off whilst the buffer beams were prepared.

The buffer beams used in this model were from my spares' box (see Fig. 283). I am not sure where they originated from, but they were plastic and of the correct pattern for use on this model, so that was deemed to be good enough. The ends of the buffer beams were trimmed to an angle of 45 degrees to match the profile on the prototype, as shown in the accompanying photographs.

The buffer mounting plate details on the buffer beams were removed with a fine file and then the holes drilled out with a 2mm bit to accept the buffers. I used ABS white metal GWR pre-Group wagon buffers, which required very little cleaning up straight from the packet. Coupling hooks from the cattle wagon kit were also installed at this stage. Once completed the buffer beams were then affixed to the ends of the wagon floors and alignment checked with the sole bars and floor to ensure all was square. I find the use of a glass tile an excellent aid in checking that everything is level and square.

ADDING THE PROTOTYPE DETAIL

When the underframe section had hardened off, I then started the construction of the sides and ends using square-section plastic microstrip as the first layer all the way round the floor section. Then on each end I added a further two layers of the square-section microstrip (see Fig. 285). On the sides I used 2mm-wide microstrip glued along its edge on top of the square section, giving a side height of approximately 3mm. I then used plasticard to form the ramps on each end of the wagon and to form the plates and support brackets over each buffer as shown in the accompanying photographs. Hanging vacuum pipes were then added using ABS white metal examples, cut from the sprue and carefully bent to shape to match the prototype.

The prototype photographs show that each wagon was equipped with two wooden wheel chocking beams and a selection of chains and/or ropes to secure the loads on the wagons. To reproduce these elements of the prototype in 4mm scale, I decided to make use of a couple of standard matchsticks for the beams. At approximately 2mm square these are a fair representation of the wooden beams, so I cut the head off each match and trimmed to length to fit snugly between the side beams of the wagon. I used fine chain to represent the load anchoring equipment.

The whole wagon was painted in GWR wagon grey and the brake lever handles picked out in white, as well as the marker line on the sole bar for the centre-line of the wagon. The wooden wheel chocking beams were painted chocolate brown and then weathered to represent well-seasoned and aged timbers.

HMRS Pressfix transfers were added to complete the model and you will see that I have used the 'Serpent.C' telegraph code to represent a pre-1943

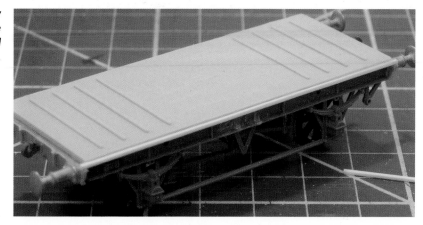

Fig. 285 The upper body sides to the wagon were minimal and on the model fabricated from microstrip.

Fig. 286 Ramps were formed from more plasticard sheet and the wooden chocking beams were formed from matches with the heads removed.

Fig. 287   The standard GWR freight livery applied and load chains added. In this figure the wagon has been fitted with decals depicting a pre-1943 livery as 'Serpent C'.

Fig. 288   The same wagon could also be updated using alternative decals to a post-1943 livery as 'CARFIT'.

model, as shown in Fig. 287. Those familiar with the HMRS sheets will know that this code is not reproduced ready formed and has to be made up by the cutting of individual letters from other codes reproduced on the sheet. For later (post-1943) models this would read 'CARFIT', as per the photographs in Russell (1971) and shown in Fig. 288.

I believe the model is a fair representation in 4mm scale of this prototype using the parts I had available, but I accept it is not a 100 per cent accurate reproduction and there were some compromises in order to get the overall look of the wagon in model form. I am extremely pleased with the result and I hope that these notes and the accompanying photographs provide a useful guide to the production of a model of this prototype, something that is not (to my knowledge) available in RTR and which can be reproduced relatively easily and quickly from commercially available parts, bits of plasticard and microstrip and a couple of matchsticks!

OTHER EXAMPLES OF SCRATCH BUILD PROJECTS

Another example of rolling stock that I have built, which could be loosely called scratch building, is to use a standard available wagon kit and to reproduce a private owner wagon livery local to the area in which my model layout is generally set. The wagon shown in Fig. 289 is an example using a Slater's unbranded private owner wagon kit, to which I have applied the livery of John Lloyd Peate and Sons. The wagon livery is based on the livery shown on one of their narrow gauge wagons running on the Welshpool and Llanfair Light Railway (Cartwright and Russell 1981), but I understand that they also ran standard gauge wagons in a similar livery style.

I have not confined my scratch building projects to OO gauge rolling stock and have over the years constructed bridges and buildings (see Figs 290 and 291), as well as narrow gauge rolling stock for my

Fig. 289 A slight variation on the theme of scratch building here with a Slater's Plastikard private owner wagon with 'scratch' livery and lettering to represent a private owner wagon local to the area of my layout. Lettering was made up using HMRS Pressfix sheets.

layout, which is in part dual gauge. The narrow gauge rolling stock has been built using parts from Ratio four-wheel coach kits for the passenger stock, whilst all of the freight stock has been scratch built using good quality card, specifically recycled business cards, running on PECO N gauge chassis kits (see Fig. 292). I have also scratch built narrow gauge locomotives and railcars using plasticard bodies running on commercially available RTR N gauge chassis, as shown in Fig. 293. All of these have been built using the skills initially developed from OO gauge rolling stock construction.

In addition to the railway prototypes described above, I have also completed a scratch built model of a small cargo ship to 4mm scale, loosely based on a Scottish Puffer, for the harbour on a friend's extensive OO gauge layout (see Fig. 294). The model ship was constructed as a water-line model to sit against a quayside. The base of the ship was formed from a sheet of 2mm plywood shaped to the correct profile section through the ship. The hull and upper deck was subsequently formed from laminated layers of card, with internal cross bracing bulk heads in the hull to provide strength, just like a real ship.

A cargo hold with removable covers was provided using thin balsawood for the hatch edge and covers. The accommodation block and wheel house at the stern was also constructed from the same material (see Fig. 295). The mast was formed from a thin dowel rod, with thin wire to represent the rigging, whilst the funnel was formed from a cut down metal tube from an old set of hair curling tongs that happened to be just the right size (see Fig. 296).

Fig. 290 Scratch building for your model railway layout need not be confined to the rolling stock. This example is a factory office built from Wills embossed plasticard sheets, suitably painted, detailed and weathered.

Fig. 291   This scratch built stone warehouse was formed from Slater's Plastikard embossed stone and roof slate sheets. A full-size mock-up of this building was produced first in plain card to get the wall and roof angles right. The doors and windows are leftovers from Ratio and Wills kits.

Fig. 292   As well as the standard gauge rolling stock, examples from the author's layout also include scratch built narrow gauge (OO9) wagon and van rolling stock formed from card bodies on PECO N gauge wagon chassis.

Fig. 293   The narrow gauge rolling stock also includes a scratch built freelance steam railcar running on N gauge Tomix Bo-Bo chassis. The body is entirely made from plasticard with staples for the hand rails.

Fig. 294　On a nautical theme, the author's scratch building skills have also been put to use to provide a small ship for a colleague's layout. In this case the ship is loosely based on a Scottish 'Puffer' and is shown moored at the quayside with the hatch cover removed and awaiting loading.

The only ready-made items used on the model were the plastic railings around the deck at the stern (from a Ratio kit), the fine chain for the anchor and the white metal crew figures from Dart Castings.

As you can appreciate from the examples described here, the opportunity to utilize your scratch building modelling skills need not be limited to just the rolling stock for your layout. The skills are transferrable to scenic development, as well as other scales, gauges and subjects.

Fig. 295　The wheelhouse is formed from a combination of balsa wood and plasticard (including the life buoy!), whilst the funnel was originally the inside tube from a pair of curling tongs! The Captain is a painted Dart Casting's figure.

Fig. 296　A stern view of the Puffer showing the laminated card hull rudder gear. The hand rails are a propriety item from the Ratio Models' range, suitably adapted for the maritime location.

SCALE 4MM:1FT CONVERSION TABLE

Inch	Foot	Yard	Mile	Scale (mm)	Comments
1	0.09	0.03	0.0001	0.36	
2	0.17	0.06	0.0001	0.68	
3	0.25	0.09	0.0001	1	
4	0.34	0.12	0.0001	1.36	
5	0.42	0.14	0.0001	1.68	
6	0.50	0.17	0.0001	2	
7	0.59	0.20	0.0002	2.36	
8	0.67	0.23	0.0002	2.68	
9	0.75	0.25	0.0002	3	
10	0.84	0.28	0.0002	3.36	
11	0.92	0.31	0.0002	3.68	
12	1.00	0.34	0.0002	4	
15	1.25	0.42	0.0003	5	
18	1.50	0.50	0.0003	6	Represents prototype 18in-gauge industrial railways
24	2.00	0.67	0.0004	8	
30	2.50	0.84	0.0005	10	Represents prototype 2ft 6in narrow gauge
36	3.00	1.00	0.0006	12	Represents prototype 3ft narrow gauge
48	4.00	1.34	0.0008	16	
49.5	4.13	1.38	0.0008	16.5	OO track gauge
56.5	4.71	1.57	0.0009	18.83	Represents prototype UK Standard Gauge; 4mm fine-scale P4
60	5.00	1.67	0.0010	20	
63	5.25	1.75	0.0010	21	Represents prototype Irish Standard Gauge
72	6	2.00	0.0012	24	
84	7	2.34	0.0014	28	

Inch	Foot	Yard	Mile	Scale (mm)	Comments
84.25	7.02	2.35	0.0014	28.08	Represents prototype Brunel Broad Gauge
96	8	2.67	0.0016	32	
108	9	3.00	0.0018	36	
120	10	3.34	0.0019	40	Represents prototype RCH 10ft wagon wheelbase
132	11	3.67	0.0021	44	
144	12	4.00	0.0023	48	
156	13	4.34	0.0025	52	
168	14	4.67	0.0027	56	
180	15	5.00	0.0029	60	
192	16	5.34	0.0031	64	
204	17	5.67	0.0033	68	
216	18	6.00	0.0035	72	
228	19	6.34	0.0037	76	
240	20	6.67	0.0038	80	
300	25	8.34	0.0048	100	
360	30	10.00	0.0057	120	
420	35	11.67	0.0067	140	
540	45	15.00	0.0086	180	
600	50	16.67	0.0095	200	
660	55	18.34	0.0105	220	
720	60	20.00	0.0114	240	
762	63.50	21.17	0.0121	254	Represents prototype 63ft 6in BR MK 1 gang-wayed coach
780	65	21.67	0.0124	260	
840	70	23.34	0.0133	280	
900	75	25.00	0.0143	300	
960	80	26.67	0.0152	320	
1,020	85	28.34	0.0162	340	
1,080	90	30.00	0.0171	360	

Inch	Foot	Yard	Mile	Scale (mm)	Comments
1,140	95	31.67	0.0180	380	
1,200	100	33.34	0.0190	400	
2,400	200	66.67	0.0379	800	
3,600	300	100.00	0.0569	1200	
4,800	400	133.34	0.0758	1600	
6,000	500	166.67	0.0947	2000	
7,200	600	200.00	0.1137	2400	
8,400	700	233.34	0.1326	2800	
9,600	800	266.67	0.1516	3200	
10,800	900	300.00	0.1705	3600	
12,000	1000	333.34	0.1894	4000	
15,840	1320	440.00	0.2500	5280	
31,680	2640	880.00	0.5000	10560	
47,520	3960	1320.00	0.7500	15840	
63,360	5280	1760.00	1.0000	21120	A scale mile!

LIST OF MATERIAL AND COMPONENT SUPPLIERS

The following list of suppliers shows the ones that I have used for component parts and raw materials when constructing and detailing kits, undertaking kit conversions and scratch building. The list is not exhaustive, as there are many more suppliers of components and materials. It is important to note that I have no connection with the suppliers listed below, other than as a satisfied customer.

51L Models / Wizard Models
Wizard Models
PO Box 70
Barton upon Humber
DN18 5XY
T: +44 (0) 1652 635885
E: Andrew@modelsignals.com
www.wizardmodels.co.uk
White metal kits and components; brass kits

ABS Models
Mail Order Dept
39 Napier Road
Hamworthy
Poole
Dorset
BH15 4LX
T: +44 (0) 1202 672891
White metal components, including buffers, coupling hooks, vacuum pipes, brake cylinders

Alan Gibson Ltd
PO Box 597
Oldham
OL1 9FQ
T: +44 (0) 161 678 1607
F: +44 (0) 161 785 8208
E: sales@alangibsonworkshop.com
www.alangibsonworkshop.com
Fine-scale OO gauge metal rolling stock wheels; sprung buffer kits for wagons and vans

Cambrian Models
10 Long Road
Tydd Gote
Wisbech
PE13 5RB
T: +44 (0) 1945 420511
E: via webpage link
www.cambrianmodels.co.uk
Plastic wagon and van kits; plastic bogie kits

Comet Models
As of December 2014 Comet Models became part of Wizard Models; *see* 51L Models above
Etched brass bogie kits; wagon and carriage components

Cooper Craft
Broom Lane
Oake
Taunton
TA4 1BE
T: +44 (0) 1823 461961
E: via web page link
www.cooper-craft.co.uk
Plastic wagon and van kits; plastic wagon and van components and underframe kits

Dart Castings
17 Hurst Close
Staplehurst
Tonbridge
Kent
TN12 0BX
T: +44 (0) 1580 892917
E: enquiries@dartcastings.co.uk
www.dartcastings.co.uk
White metal components; white metal figures

Falcon Brassworks
Same address as Dart Castings
T: +44 (0) 1580 892917
E: enquiries@falconbrassworks.com
www.falconbrassworks.com
Etched brass wagon and van kits

Fox Transfers Ltd
4 Hill Lane Close
Markfield Ind Estate
Markfield
Leicestershire
LE67 9PN
T: +44 (0) 1530 245618
E: sales@fox-transfers.co.uk
www.fox-transfers.co.uk
Waterslide transfers

Historical Model Railway Society (HMRS)
HMRS Museum and Study Centre
Midland Railway Centre
Butterley Railway Station
Ripley
DE5 3QZ
T: +44 (0) 1773 745 959
E: via web page link
www.hmrs.org.uk
Pressfix freight, passenger stock and locomotive insignia

K and S Metals
Distributed in the UK by:
J Perkins Distribution Ltd
Northdown Business Park
Ashford Road
Lenham
Kent
ME17 2DL
T: +44 (0) 1622 854 300
F: +44 (0) 1622 854 301
E: sales@jpmodels.co.uk
www.ksmetals.com
Brass sheet and rod

Mainly Trains
PO Box 50
Watchet
Somerset
TA23 0WQ
T: +44 (0) 1278 741333
E: web@mainlytrains.co.uk
www.mainlytrains.co.uk
White metal, turned brass and etched brass components

Markits / Romford
Markits
PO Box 40
Watford
Hertfordshire
WD24 6TN
T: +44 (0) 1923 249711
www.markits.com
Turned brass components / fine scale OO gauge metal rolling stock wheels

Parkside Dundas
Millie Street
Kirkcaldy
Fife
KY1 2NL
T: +44 (0) 1592 640896
E: via web page link
www.parksidedundas.co.uk
Plastic wagon and van kits; fine metal chain

PECO
PECO Technical Advice Bureau
Underleys
Beer
Devon
EX12 3NA
T: +44 (0) 1297 21542
F: +44 (0) 1297 20229
E: info@pecobeer.co.uk
www.peco-uk.com
Plastic wagon kits

Phoenix Precision Paints Ltd
Orwell Court
Wickford
Essex
SS11 8YJ
T: 01268 730549
E: sales@phoenix-paints.co.uk
www.phoenix-paints.co.uk
Authentic railway company colour enamel paints

Plastruct
Available from model shops
Extruded plastic components

Ratio Models
Distributed by PECO, *see above*
Plastic wagon and van kits; plastic bogie kits

Roxey Mouldings
58 Dudley Road
Walton-on-Thames
Surrey
KT12 2JU
T: +44 (0) 1932 245439
E: dave@roxeymouldings.co.uk
www.roxeymouldings.co.uk
Turned brass components; white metal and brass kits

Shire Scenes
The Old Armoury
North Street
Somerton
Somerset
TA11 7NY
T: +44 (0) 1458 272446
E: order@shirescenes.co.uk
www.shirescenes.co.uk
Etched brass part kits for conversion of Ratio four-wheel coach kits

Slater's Plastikard Ltd
Old Road
Darley Dale
Matlock
Derbyshire
DE4 2ER
T: +44 (0) 1629 734053
F: +44 (0) 1629 732235
E: slaters@slatersplastikard.com
www.slatersplastikard.com
Range of plain and embossed plasticard in varying thicknesses; microstrip and plastic rod

Ten Commandments
20 Struan Drive
Inverkeithing
Fife
KY11 1AR
T: 01383 410032
E: tencommandments@cast-in-stone.co.uk
www.cast-in-stone.co.uk
Range of stone cast wagon loads for painting

BIBLIOGRAPHY

The following list of books and articles has been used as reference material in the preparation of this book:

Atkins, A. G., Beard, W. and Tourret, R. *GWR Goods Wagons – A Historical Survey* (Oxford Publishing Co., V), 2013

Beck, K. M. *The West Midland Lines of the GWR* (Ian Allan Ltd, 1983)

Beck, K. M. *The Great Western North of Wolverhampton* (Ian Allan Ltd, 1986)

Beck, K. M. and Harris, N. *GWR Reflections* (Silver Link Publishing Ltd, 1987)

Booth, T. J. *Modeller's Guide to the GWR* (Patrick Stephens Ltd, 1990)

Cartwright, R. and Russell, R. T. *The Welshpool and Llanfair Light Railway* (David and Charles, 1981)

Green, C. C. *Cambrian Railways 1859–1947 Combined Edition* (Ian Allan Ltd, 1997)

Lavey, K. R. 'Scratch Build of a Mink F', *Model Railway Constructor* (volume 51, number 606, October 1984, pp. 514–516)

Mitchell, V. and Smith, K. *Branch Lines Around Oswestry (Gobowen, Tanat Valley, Llanfyllin and Welshpool)* (Middleton Press, 2009)

Prideaux, J. D. C. A. *The Welsh Narrow Gauge Railway – A Pictorial History* (David and Charles, 1982)

Russell, J. H. *A Pictorial Record of Great Western Wagons* (Oxford Publishing Co., 1971)

Russell, J. H. *Great Western Wagons Appendix – A Further Selection of GWR Wagons and Cranes* (Oxford Publishing Co., 1974)

Russell, J. H. *A Pictorial Record of Great Western Coaches (Part One 1838–1913) Including the Brown Vehicles* (Oxford Publishing Co., 1979)

Russell, J. H. *Freight Wagons and Loads in Service on the Great Western Railway and British Rail, Western Region* (Oxford Publishing Co., 1981)

Russell, J. H. *A Pictorial Record of Great Western Coaches (Part Two 1903–1948) Including the Brown Vehicles* (Oxford Publishing Co., 1990)

Tisdale, D. C. 'GWR Cordon Gas Tank Wagon – a special internal use wagon from the days of gas lit carriages', *Railway Modeller* (volume 61, number 711, January 2010a, pp. 50–51)

Tisdale, D. C. 'Great Western four-wheel parcels van – an easy conversion of the Ratio 610 all third coach kit in 4mm scale', *Railway Modeller* (volume 61, number 721, November 2010b, pp. 860–861)

Tisdale, D. C. 'GWR Small Mex – constructing a cattle wagon variant in 4mm scale', *Railway Modeller* (volume 62, number 726, April 2011a, pp. 264–265)

Tisdale, D. C. 'GWR Serpent – a flat wagon for special loads in 4mm scale', *Railway Modeller* (volume 62, number 730, August 2011b, pp. 604–605)

Tisdale, D. C. 'GWR Short Python – a conversion for a Parkside Dundas kit in 4mm scale', *Railway Modeller* (volume 63, number 737, March 2012a, pp. 232–233)

Tisdale, D. C. 'Alternative Toads – GWR brake van modelling in 4mm scale', *Railway Modeller* (volume 63, number 740, June 2012b, pp. 524–525)

Tisdale, D. C. 'A Short Toad – another brake van conversion in 4mm scale', *Railway Modeller* (volume 63, number 743, September 2012c, pp. 814–815)

Tisdale, D. C. 'Six-wheel Toad – Another GW brake van conversion in 4mm scale', *Railway Modeller* (volume 64, number 748, February 2013, pp. 112–113)

Tisdale, D. C. 'Scratchbuilding a Tourn', *Railway Modeller* (volume 65, number 766, August 2014, pp. 632–635)

Williams, C. L. *Great Western Steam in Wales and the Border Counties* (D. Bradford Barton Ltd, 1974)

Williams, C. L. *Great Western Branch Line Steam* (D. Bradford Barton Ltd, 1976)

INDEX